NELSON SCIENCE

# Teacher's Classroom Manual

KEY STAGE 2

Stephen Hopkins
Mary Jowett

Nelson

**Thomas Nelson and Sons Ltd**
Nelson House Mayfield Road
Walton-on-Thames Surrey
KT12 5PL UK

51 York Place
Edinburgh
EH1 3JD UK

**Thomas Nelson (Hong Kong) Ltd**
Toppan Building 10/F
22A Westlands Road
Quarry Bay Hong Kong

**Thomas Nelson Australia**
102 Dodds Street
South Melbourne
Victoria 3205
Australia

**Nelson Canada**
1120 Birchmount Road
Scarborough Ontario
M1K 5G4 Canada



First published by Thomas Nelson and Sons Ltd in co-operation with Bishop Grosseteste College, Lincoln, 1991

ISBN 0–17–423201 – 2
NPN 9 8 7 6 5 4 3 2 1



Printed in Hong Kong
The authors and publishers are grateful to the following for their help in the preparation of this manual:

Cheswick Green Infant and Junior School,
Cheswick Green, Solihull
Heath Mount Junior and Infant School, Sparkbrook, Birmingham
Kings Heath Junior School, Kings Heath, Birmingham
Kingsbury First School, Kingsbury, Warwickshire
Marlborough Junior School, Small Heath, Birmingham
Meadow Green Infant and Junior School,
Selly Oak, Birmingham
Mill Lodge Infant and Junior School, Shirley, Solihull
Whitford Hall School, Bromsgrove, Worcestershire

The Birmingham Botanical Gardens, Edgbaston, Birmingham

Clare Benson, Senior Lecturer, Faculty of Education,
Birmingham Polytechnic, Edgbaston, Birmingham

The extracts from *Science in the National Curriculum* are reproduced with the permission of the Controller of Her Majesty's Stationery Office.

All photographs by Chris Ridgers

Cover illustration by Tom Saecker

# Contents

# Introduction

The purpose of this manual is to provide support for the teacher in planning and implementing science in the curriculum of 7-11 year-olds **(Key Stage 2: Levels 2–5)**.

Planning a scheme of work to span these years will mean ensuring that children have a broad range of learning opportunities. This range is necessary for them to:

- cover the **Programmes of Study** laid down in the **National Curriculum**
- demonstrate progression in learning as mapped out by the **Attainment Targets and Levels**

All children will be working towards **Attainment Target 1, Exploration of science,** whenever they are engaged in scientific investigations. The **Attainment Targets** for **Knowledge and understanding,** however, are context-related, and the school will need to provide a progressive, broad and balanced range of contexts to give children the necessary range of learning opportunities.

This manual is a flexible resource which provides:

- frameworks to support the identification and enhancement of science learning opportunities within programmes of work (such as topics and cross-curricular themes)
- a range of scientific investigations grouped into themes and units; these are closely matched to the **National Curriculum** and provide opportunities for children to reach **Level 5** within **Attainment Target 1** and other relevant **Attainment Targets (2–17)**
- support for teachers in providing children with a broad and balanced range of experiences that will promote the development of their knowledge and understanding of science and the skills for its exploration

The *Nelson Science Teacher's Classroom Manual (Key Stage 1)* has been developed to provide a resource of activities for children who are attaining wholly or mainly within **Levels 1** and **2,** extending to **Level 3**.

*The Teacher's Classroom Manual (Key Stage 2)* builds on this foundation and provides a resource of activities notionally for **Levels 2 to 5**.

**Section 1** gives an overview of the themes and units which comprise Section 2. Ways in which the units can be used to plan and implement science within the curriculum are described and the framework for teaching and learning which is used to structure each unit is explained in detail.

The framework has been devised to help the teacher plan, organise, manage and evaluate science learning opportunities in a wide range of classroom settings. It would be appropriate to read this general section before turning to the specific guidance and support for each of the units which make up Section 2.

**Section 2** comprises thirteen units. In each unit the relationship between learning opportunities, the **National Curriculum** and the child's experience is clearly demonstrated. The guidance in each unit is structured according to the framework for teaching and learning outlined in Section 1.

**Section 3** provides detailed guidance on planning science in the context of an integrated primary curriculum. The procedure outlined here will ensure that the children experience balanced and progressive coverage of the **National Curriculum** in science, and that scientific learning experiences can be provided for children as part of a cross-curricular approach.

-notes for teachers; planning and teaching science in relation to the National Curriculum

-a range of carefully selected pictorial material; notes and references to Attainment Targets are included

-to support children's scientific exploration and investigation

-notes for teachers; assessing performance according to National Curriculum criteria

| The Nelson Science materials | |
|---|---|
| Key Stage 1 | Key Stage 2 |
| Teacher's Classroom Manual | Teacher's Classroom Manual |
| Picture Resource Books 1, 2, 3 | |
| Science Explorers 1<br>Carrying out Surveys 1<br>Experimenting 1<br>Problem Solving 1<br>Teacher's Guide to Science Explorers 1 | Science Explorers 2, 3<br>*Carrying out Surveys 2,3*<br>*Experimenting 2, 3*<br>*Problem Solving 2,3*<br>*Teacher's Notes* |
| Nelson Science Assessments | Nelson Science Assessments |

# Section 1
# Themes and Units

## Overview

Science is essentially about finding out through first-hand experience.

In *Nelson Science*, the **National Curriculum Attainment Targets** relating to **Knowledge and understanding of science** have been grouped into ten 'finding out' themes. Each theme may embrace one or more units (see below).

| THEME | UNIT |
|---|---|
| Light | Colour, mirrors, lenses and prisms |
| Sound | Noise and music |
| Batteries, buzzers and bulbs | Circuits, switching and control |
| How people change the environment | The local environment and beyond |
| Themselves and others and how to keep healthy | Our bodies |
| Plants | How flowering plants work |
| | Living things in the local environment |
| Animals | How animals work |
| Sky and weather | Measuring the weather |
| | Our solar system |
| Moving things | Movement, forces and energy |
| Materials | Weathering, minerals, rocks and soil |
| | Everyday materials |

These units cover the full range of learning opportunities in the **Programmes of Study** and the full range of **Attainment Targets** relating to **Knowledge and understanding:**

| THEME | ATTAINMENT TARGETS FOR KEY STAGE 2 | | | | | | | | | | | | | |
|---|---|---|---|---|---|---|---|---|---|---|---|---|---|---|
| | 1 | 2 | 3 | 4 | 5 | 6 | 9 | 10 | 11 | 12 | 13 | 14 | 15 | 16 |
| Light | • | | | | | | | | | • | • | | • | |
| Sound | • | | | | • | | | | | • | | • | | |
| Batteries, buzzers and bulbs | • | | | | | | | | • | • | | | | |
| How people change the environment | • | | | | • | • | | | | • | | | | |
| Themselves and others and how to keep healthy | • | | • | • | | | | | | • | • | | | |
| Plants | • | • | • | • | • | | | | | • | | | | |
| Animals | • | • | • | • | • | | | | | • | | | | |
| Sky and weather | • | | | | | | • | | | • | | | | • |
| Moving things | • | | | | | | | • | | • | • | | | |
| Materials | • | | | | | • | • | • | | • | • | | | |

This table shows the major links between the units.
Guidance on other possible links are given in each unit.

## Progression and continuity with the *Teacher's Classroom Manual (Key Stage 1)*

**Continuity** is provided across the two **Key Stages** through the use of the same organising framework:

- The same ten broad themes are used to organise the content.
- The activities within the units subsumed by the themes are based on the same three colour-coded question stems.
- Evaluation checklists are always provided on photocopiable pages at the end of each unit.
- Photocopiable planning/record sheets are provided.

**Progression** from **Key Stage 1** to **Key Stage 2** has been recognised:

- The number and nature of the units subsumed by each theme have been changed.
- The activities for **Key Stage 2** will enable children to attain within **Levels 3** to **5**. Teachers who require details of the **Levels 1** and **2** investigations will need to consult the *Teacher's Classroom Manual (Key Stage 1).*

## Using the themes and units

The units can be used to support a variety of approaches to planning and implementing science within the **Key Stage 2** curriculum.

### Approach A

The potential for science-related learning opportunities within cross-curricular topics and themes can be accessed:

– using the planning procedure outlined in Section 3. For example, a topic on festivals will provide opportunities for children to find out about Unit 1: Light, Unit 2: Sound and Unit 13: Materials. Help with record keeping, if this approach is adopted, is given in Section 3.

– through the suggestions for topics provided at the start of each unit (and gathered together in the Index on page 195).

### Approach B

Programmes of work can be structured in terms of units. For example, a school may plan to teach one unit every half term, enabling each unit to be revisited at least twice in four years. Help with record keeping, if this approach is adopted, is given in Section 3.

### Approach C

The units can be used as a resource of ideas to extend and enhance the science curriculum, whatever approach to planning and record keeping is adopted by the school and the teacher. To facilitate this approach the **Attainment Targets** covered by each group of units are shown in the chart on page 2.

The vocabulary which may be appropriate for the Key Stage 2 units is summarised in Appendix B.

## The structure of the units

The thirteen units which comprise Section 2 follow the same pattern. They are grouped by theme, and every unit has the theme symbol on each page. On pages 4–10 a model unit is outlined, with explanatory notes under each heading, as a framework for teaching and learning.

# UNIT TITLE

## Opportunities for learning

A summary of the contents of the unit, closely related to the **Programme of Study** for **Key Stage 2**.

Before starting work the teacher is strongly advised to read the checklist for teaching which is one of the photocopiable sheets at the end of each unit.

## Topics

Suggested cross-curricular topics within which the investigations contained within the unit could be embedded.

## Cross-curricular links

Brief suggestions for links with areas of the curriculum.

## Classroom materials

The *Nelson Science* materials which support the unit.

## Related units

Some of the other units within this manual which the teacher might use when planning sequences of work or when responding to the direction in which the children take the work.

Appropriate units in the **Key Stage 1** manual which provide the foundation for work in the unit. This is especially important where the teacher has children working within **Levels 1** and **2.**

## Resources and equipment

Guidance on the resources and equipment that are likely to be used by children carrying out the investigations in the unit.

## Safety

Advice and guidance to raise awareness about possible hazards associated with work in the unit.

We recommend that all schools have copies of the following:

*Be Safe: Some Aspects of Safety in Science and Technology in Primary Schools* (Association for Science Education 1988, 1990)

'Animals and plants in schools: legal aspects'

(DES Memorandum March 1990)

## Starting points

Suggestions which set the work of the unit within the child's experience are organised under three broad headings: 'The school environment', 'The social environment' and 'Further afield'.

In *Nelson Science*, **Attainment Target 1** is divided into three parts:

- **asking questions** and suggesting ideas about materials and events
- **gathering information** through first-hand experience
- **handling information** that has been gathered, by recording and interpreting findings

This framework underpins the first-hand practical investigations in which the children engage.

This diagram shows how these three aspects of science exploration were derived from the **Programme of Study** for **Attainment Target 1.**

**Asking questions**
- promote the raising and answering of questions
- encourage the formulation of testable hypotheses

**Gathering information**
- provide opportunities to explore with increasing precision, where appropriate
- require the development of an increasingly systematic approach involving the indentification and manipulation of obvious key variables
- develop skills of using equipment and measurement, encouraging children to make decisions about when, what, and how to measure
- encourage a working understanding of safety and care

**Exploration of science**
Key Stage 2: Attainment Target 1

**Handling information**
- encourage the systematic listing and recording of data, for example, in frequency tables and bar charts
- encourage the searching for patterns in data
- encourage the interpretation of data, and evaluation against the demands of the problem
- encourage the development of written and / or oral reporting skills, as appropriate
- encourage the use of a limited technical vocabulary in communicating findings and ideas

The following three diagrams show how the **Statements of Attainment** for **Attainment Target 1** relate to the three component parts.

**Level 2**
- ask questions and suggest ideas of the 'how', 'why' and 'what will happen if ' variety

**Level 3**
- formulate hypotheses

**Asking questions**
- promote the raising and answering of questions
- encourage the formulation of testable hypotheses

**Level 4**
- raise questions in a form which can be investigated
- formulate testable hypotheses

**Level 5**
- suggest simple questions for investigation

**Level 2**
- use non-standard and standard measures
- identify simple differences, for example, hot / cold, rough / smooth

**Level 3**
- select and use simple instruments to enhance observations
- quantify variables, as appropriate, to the nearest labelled division of simple measuring instruments, for example, a ruler
- identify, and describe simple variables that change over time, for example, growth of a plant
- distinguish between a 'fair' and an 'unfair' test

**Gathering information**
- provide opportunities to explore with increasing precision, where appropriate
- require the development of an increasingly systematic approach involving the identification and manipulation of obvious key variables
- develop skills of using equipment and measurement, encouraging children to make decisions about when, what and how to measure
- encourage a working understanding of safety and care

**Level 4**
- interpret written instructions and diagrammatic representations
- plan and safely carry out an investigation where the plan indicates that the relevant variables have been identified and others controlled
- construct 'fair tests'
- select and use a range of measuring instruments, as appropriate, to quantify observations of physical quantities, such as volume and temperature

**Level 5**
- use simple concepts, knowledge and skills in the design of an investigation
- identify and manipulate relevant independent and dependent variables, choosing appropriately ranges, numbers and values
- select and use measuring instruments to quantify variables and use more complex measuring instruments with required degree of accuracy, such as minor divisions on ammeters and forcemeters

**Level 2**
- list and collate observations
- record findings in charts, drawings and other appropriate forms
- interpret findings by associating one factor with another, for example, 'light objects float'

**Level 3**
- record experimental findings, for example in tables and bar charts
- interpret simple pictograms and bar charts
- interpret observations in terms of a generalised statement
- describe activities carried out by sequencing the major features

**Handling information**
- encourage the systematic listing and recording of data, for example, in frequency tables and bar charts
- encourage the searching for patterns in data
- encourage the interpretation of data, and evaluation against the demands of the problem
- encourage the development of written and / or oral reporting skills, as appropriate
- encourage the use of a limited technical vocabulary in communicating findings and ideas

**Level 4**
- record results by the construction of simple tables, bar charts,pie charts and line graphs, as appropriate
- draw conclusions from experimental results
- describe investigations in the form of ordered prose, using a limited technical vocabulary

**Level 5**
- use simple concepts, knowledge and skills in the interpretation of results
- make written statements of the patterns derived from the data obtained from various sources

## Asking questions

Asking questions is a fundamental aspect of developing an understanding of the environment. It is the means by which children find out the information they need to help them understand. The questions children ask show where their existing ideas are not adequate to interpret their new experiences. They represent the gaps which have to be filled before a new experience can be fitted into, or used to challenge, existing notions.

Children should be encouraged to ask all kinds of questions, to help them to form links between previous and new experiences and so enlarge understanding. The complex 'how' and 'why' explanation-seeking questions should be encouraged in **Key Stage 2**. To help children to reach the point where they can raise questions in a form which can be investigated, the investigations included in each unit are grouped under three question stems:

**I wonder whether ...**

**What happens if ...**

**Can I find a way to ...**

Many forms of question are, of course, appropriate. These three particular question stems provide powerful organisers of children's work as they inherently indicate three broad types of science activity.

If they are used in discussions before and during investigations, printed on displays and used when children are making recordings, they will help children to formulate their thinking in terms of investigable questions.

A sample of investigable questions is included in each unit. There are of course many more questions which are applicable to each unit. Those offered are ideas to stimulate and support teachers when planning.

It is not intended that teachers/children should complete every investigation. The teacher will need to choose those which are most appropriate for their particular circumstances and which achieve a balance across the three broad aspects identified.

Section 3 of this manual provides guidance to help the teacher ensure that there is a balanced coverage of the **Programme of Study** across the four years of **Key Stage 2.**

## Gathering information

### Carrying out surveys

Carrying out a survey involves children in observing, recording and grouping the key characteristics of objects and events; in other words, it involves them in looking for relationships.

**'I wonder whether ...'** questions tend to lead children to carry out surveys.

### Experimenting

Simple experiments involve the child in changing variables and observing effects.

**'What happens if ...'** questions tend to lead children to experiment.

### Solving practical problems

Practical problems can be used as a stimulus and motivation for carrying out surveys and experimenting, or children can use skills and concepts gained in these ways to solve practical problems.

**'Can I find a way to ...'** questions lead children to try to solve practical problems.

## Handling information

Children's scientific activities should give them opportunities to use and develop a range of communication skills and techniques. In addition to the oral work before, during and after practical activity, children will be involved in making records of their findings through drawings, charts, three-dimensional models, and the written word.

Each unit includes examples of ways in which children can appropriately record findings. The examples given are closely related to the **National Curriculum Programme of Study** and to **Attainment Target 1 (Exploration of science)** Only a sample of the range of recording methods which enhance children's experience are given within the confines of each unit.

## Review points

Discussion following practical experience is a crucial means through which learning is supported, consolidated and extended.

### Our investigations

This section provides the teacher with a suggested (technical) vocabulary which may be used during the work on the unit. Questions which can form the basis of valuable discussion are also listed. (The vocabulary lists for all the units are summarised in Appendix B.)

### Making connections

This section raises discussion points which will help children to make links between the ideas and experiences built into the unit and to relate their classroom activities to a broader context of phenomena and ideas.

## Investigations

This section extends the help available from the question stems under the headings 'Asking questions' and 'Gathering information'. The investigations which might follow from the sample of questions in each unit are described using photographs where appropriate to aid clarity.

## Evaluation checklists

Each unit ends with two photocopiable evaluation checklists.

This sample unit ends with a photocopiable evaluation checklist for **Attainment Target 1** as this will be needed for each unit.

The wording of the statutory orders has been clearly adhered to but the components of the **Statements of Attainment** are separated to help clarify the requirements and to aid record keeping.

### Teaching

This checklist clarifies the parts of the **Programme of Study** which are covered by the unit.

### Learning

This checklist covers the relevant **Statements of Attainment** for **Levels 1** to **5.**

### How to use the evaluation checklists

The teacher can use each evaluation checklist as:

- a pre-activity checklist to ensure that activities are developed with a purpose. The statements in the checklist should help sharpen the focus of work in the classroom, offering children opportunities to achieve particular **Levels of Attainment.**
- a post-activity checklist to make and record evaluations of the teaching and learning.

The checklists are photocopiable and teachers should adapt this recording device to suit their own needs.

The checklists are not designed to be a substitute for recording the attainment of individual children. They are, however, a useful means of focusing on the **Statements of Attainment** which relate to the unit and of recording those statements which have been used for assessment purposes.

Detailed guidance is provided in Section 3 of this manual.

This checklist covers **Attainment Target 1 (Exploration of science)**.It should be used in relation to each of the units.

## Attainment Target 1: Evaluation Checklist

| | Level 2 | Level 3 | Level 4 | Level 5 |
|---|---|---|---|---|
| **ASKING QUESTIONS** | • ask questions and suggest ideas of the 'how','why' and 'what will happen if' variety | • formulate hypotheses, for example, *this ball will bounce higher than that one* | • raise questions in a form which can be investigated<br>• formulate testable hypotheses | • suggest simple questions for investigation |
| **GATHERING INFORMATION** | • use non-standard and standard measures, for example, *hand-spans and rulers*<br>• identify simple differences, for example, *hot / cold, rough / smooth* | • select and use simple instruments to enhance observations, for example, *a stop-clock or hand lens*<br>• quantify variables, as appropriate, to the nearest labelled division of simple measuring instruments, for example, *a ruler*<br>• identify and describe simple variables that change over time, for example, *growth of a plant*<br>• distinguish between a 'fair' and an 'unfair' test | • interpret written instructions and diagrammatic representations<br>• plan and safely carry out an investigation where the plan indicates that the relevant variables have been identified and the others controlled<br>• construct 'fair tests'<br>• select and use a range of measuring instruments, as appropriate, to quantify observations of physical quantities, such as volume and temperature | • use simple concepts, knowledge and skills in the design of an investigation<br>• identify and manipulate relevant independent and dependent variables, choosing appropriately ranges, numbers and values<br>• select and use measuring instruments to quantify variables and use more complex measuring instruments with required degree of accuracy, for example, *minor divisions on thermometers and forcemeters* |
| **HANDLING INFORMATION** | • list and collate observations<br>• record findings in charts, drawings and other appropriate forms<br>• interpret findings by associating one factor with another, for example, *light objects float, thin wood is bendy* | • record experimental findings<br>• interpret simple pictograms and bar charts<br>• interpret observations in terms of a generalised statement, for example, *the greater the suspended weight,the longer the spring*<br>• describe activities carried out by sequencing the major features | • record results by the construction of simple tables, bar charts, pie charts, line graphs, as appropriate<br>• draw conclusions from experimental results<br>• describe investigations in the form of ordered prose, using a limited technical vocabulary | • use simple concepts, knowledge and skills in the interpretation of results<br>• make written statements of the patterns derived from the data obtained from various sources |

**Attainment Target 12 Level 3**

- know that information can be stored electronically in a variety of ways, for example, *text, number, pictures and sound*
- be able to retrieve and select text, number, sound or graphics on a computer

- safety pervades all practical work

## Information Technology

Investigations are included within various units to provide opportunities for pupils to develop their knowledge and understanding of **AT12: The scientific aspects of Information Technology including micro-electronics.**

Two of the **Level 3 Statements of Attainment** are, however, of a general nature and have thus been included on the **AT1** evaluation checklist (page 11).

***Technology in the National Curriculum*** (DES and the Welsh Office 1990) contains full details of **Attainment Targets** and the **Programmes of Study** for Technology.

(Examples of data handling programs directly relevant to science are given in Appendix A.)

# Section 2
# Science Units

This section gives detailed guidance for each of the thirteen units. They are grouped by theme, and every unit has its theme symbol on each page. Each unit follows the pattern shown below and described in detail in Section 1 of this manual.

| | |
|---|---|
| Planning and Preparation | Opportunities for learning ↓ Topics ↓ Cross–curricular links ↓ Classroom materials ↓ Related units ↓ Resources ↓ |
| In the Classroom | Starting points ↓ Asking questions ↓ Gathering information ↓ Handling information ↓ Review points ↓ Investigations ↓ Evaluation checklists |

# UNIT 1
# COLOUR, MIRRORS, LENSES AND PRISMS

## Opportunities for learning

Working from this unit, children will be developing their investigative skills and their knowledge and understanding of:

- the properties and behaviour of light
- the range of energy sources and the issues involved in their exploitation

For greater detail, refer to the evaluation checklist (teaching) at the end of this unit.

## Topics

| | |
|---|---|
| **BUILDINGS** | Light to work by<br>Buildings in other countries |
| **ENERGY** | Sources, storage, generation of electricity |
| **FESTIVALS** | Shiny fabrics, reflective surfaces, periscopes |
| **OUR SCHOOL** | Blinds or blackout curtains<br>Hiding unsightly objects by painting them<br>Colour and display |
| **THE SEASONS** | Position of the sun in the sky<br>Strength of the sun |
| **TRANSPORT** | Car or bicycle lights and mirrors<br>Street 'furniture' |

## Cross-curricular links

| | |
|---|---|
| **ART** | Primary colours |
| **ENGLISH / DRAMA** | Shadow puppets |
| **GEOGRAPHY** | Energy supply and consumption |
| **MATHEMATICS** | Measuring angles, symmetry, prisms |
| **PE / MOVEMENT** | Mirror images |

## Classroom materials

The following *Nelson Science* materials support this unit:

**Picture Resource Book 1**

- cover - a rainbow
- p.12, 13 - shadows
- p.14 - reflections on water
- p.15 - the moon as a huge reflective surface

**Picture Resource Book 2**

- p.7 - the pupils' response to light
- p.6 - the use of light sources and mirrors at the dentist's surgery
- p.10 - camouflage in animals

**Picture Resource Book 3**

- p.6 - miners' use of light sources
- p.13 - the Eiffel Tower illuminated
- p.22 - a reflective surface

**Science Explorers**

- **Carrying Out Surveys 1, 2 and 3**
- **Experimenting 1, 2 and 3**
- **Problem Solving 1, 2 and 3**

## Related units

### Units in the Teacher's Classroom Manual (Key Stage 2)

- Circuits, switching and control - Unit 3
- The local environment and beyond - Unit 4
- Living things in the local environment - Unit 7
- Our solar system - Unit 10
- Movement, forces and energy - Unit 11
- Everyday materials - Unit 13

### Units in the Teacher's Classroom Manual (Key Stage 1)

- Light, shadows, colours and mirrors - Unit 1

## Resources and equipment

- torches
- lenses (old spectacle lenses)
- magnifying glasses
- prisms
- a variety of framed and unframed mirrors: flat, concave, convex, shaving, make-up, from car breakers' yards, large wall-mounted
- stands for mirrors: wood blocks, bulldog clips, egg boxes, Plasticine
- a variety of transparent containers: pyrex cooking dishes, plastic beakers (made from cutting up lemonade bottles), opaque dishes or bowls, goldfish bowls
- a variety of cardboard tubes, sheets and boxes
- paper: tissue, thick, dark
- silver foil
- combs
- dark or black cloth
- coloured acetate sheets (at least blue, red and green)
- food colourings (with droppers if required)
- bottles/ jars

## Safety

Ensure that the children:

- never direct light beams at other people's faces
- take care when storing magnifying glasses
- are reminded about the importance of reporting breakages if using glass
- do not under any circumstances look directly at the sun or other strong light sources
- use mirrors with edges protected with tape

## Starting points

### The school environment

- the need for shading on the classroom window at certain times of the year or on certain days
- in swimming lessons, the instructor's `guide' pole looks bent where it enters the water
- reflectors or fluorescent strips on bags, badges, jackets and trainers
- a rainbow in the sky

### The social environment

- the school or local disco, with its lights, sequins and shiny clothing
- bicycle light reflectors
- car lights and mirrors, warning lights and colours of emergency vehicles
- `street furniture': road signs, traffic lights, reflectors, cats' eyes
- eye-catching advertisements and shop displays
- Christmas lights
- in the low sunlight of the morning or evening, a rainbow may be seen in the spray of a garden hose, especially if it is viewed against a dark background

### Further afield

- a lighthouse
- large shopping centres - mirrors and shiny surfaces

Also see 'Making connections'.

## Asking questions

### I wonder whether ...

- **food colourings mix in the way paints do?**
- **a red tomato always looks red?**
- **hollow dish-shaped mirrors give a different image from mirrors which bulge out like a ball?**
- **I can find something which magnifies as well as a lens?**
- **everybody holds a magnifying glass the same distance from the object being observed?**

## Gathering information

### Carrying out surveys

**Children:**

- **observe and record the effect of placing one drop of food colouring at a time into a transparent container of still water**
- **collect transparent objects in different colours and observe everyday objects through them**
- **collect as many different types of mirror as they can and classify them by the images they produce**
- **experiment with, for example, small plastic bottles, clock fronts covered in clear fablon, watch glasses and water**
- **plan how to make comparisons 'fair' (which variables must stay constant) and how to record**

## Asking questions

### What happens if ...

- we turn on a torch in a dark box?
- we place objects in a torch beam?
- we place a flat mirror in light rays?
- we place a lens in light rays?
- we change the order of ROYGBIV colours in a spinner?
- we try to copy a pattern which is reflected in a mirror?

### Can I find a way to ...

- make a dark area big enough to work in?
- send a message using light?
- make a coloured shadow?
- make a giant's shadow for our puppet play?
- work out whether a mirror, large enough to see ourselves from head to toe, will fit on the bedroom wall?
- make an advertisement which stands out from the others?
- make a rainbow?
- show that light is bent by some materials?

## Gathering information

### Experimenting

Children:

- predict, then set up a torch to shine into a dark box
- experiment with opaque, transparent and translucent objects, including cardboard tubes and combs
- place a flat mirror in the sharp 'rays' coming through a comb and experiment with any other mirrors available
- experiment as above, but with a variety of lenses instead of mirrors
- (with experience of making spinners and getting them to balance well) experiment with coloured segments
- (who appreciate that mirror images are reversed) could set up puzzles for each other

### Solving practical problems

Children:

- experiment with different enclosed areas
- use a shiny surface on a sunny day (or a torch in dull weather); working in pairs, they transmit and receive messages, giving the appropriate response
- cover a torch beam with cellophane or sweet wrappers
- experiment to find, for example, that the brightest light source gives the sharpest shadows
- use a column of mirror tiles firmly attached to a convenient wall where a large mirror is inappropriate
- draw on previous experience of colours which stand out
- use a prism, thinking about what a prism is and whether it is possible to 'imitate' one
- look at straight objects through different transparent materials

Examples of ways in which these ideas have been developed in the classroom are provided on pages 19–25.

## Handling information

- Encourage systematic listing and recording of data:
  - – frequency tables
  - – bar charts
- Encourage searching for patterns in data.
- Encourage written and/or oral reporting skills as appropriate.

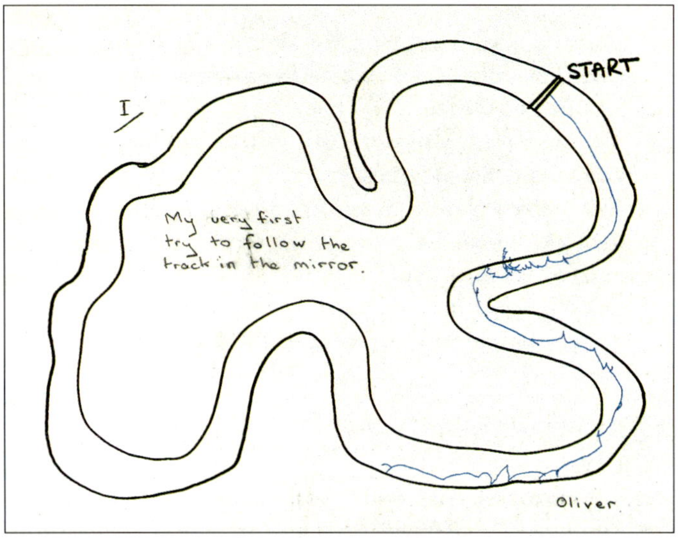


- Encourage the use of a limited technical vocabulary in communicating findings and ideas.

My periscope.

The light from the object I look at hits the top of the mirror, and is bounced back to the bottom one. Then it is bounced into my eyes. This is called reflection.

- Encourage the interpretation of data, and evaluation against the demands of the problem.

MEETINGS MEAN HATS THEN GRANDFATHER CLOCKS. STOW ERIC ON BOARD.

## Review points

The following are useful talking points:

### Our investigations

- the new vocabulary we learned; for example: *lens, magnification, prism, spectrum, ray, beam, transparent, translucent, opaque, image, represent, refraction, acetate;* can we add to our definitions?
- the questions we raised that we answered, and those we must leave unanswered
- the variables we controlled, and those we should have or would like to have controlled
- the new equipment we used, or skills we learned; were we successful? do we need more practice?
- any patterns we noticed in the data or tentative hypotheses we made

### Making connections

- the use of transparent and translucent windows
- the use of opaque things, for example, sun shields on cars to stop the light, or the blind on the classroom window
- the need to take clothes to natural light in a clothes shop to see the 'true' colour
- camouflage: in animals, in army uniforms, even decorators 'hiding' unsightly objects by painting them the same colour as the wall
- the use of mirrors, for example by an organist to see the conductor, by drivers of cars on tight corners
- the fact that swimming pools are deeper than they appear
- light – the ultimate energy source
- plants and animals which live in little light, for example liverworts and owls
- living things which do not need light, for example fungi and bats
- periscopes in submarines or to see over crowds
- satellite dishes - Jodrell Bank
- telescopes and microscopes
- moonlight - a reflection of light from the sun
- optical illusions, including the cinema and 'flick' pictures, zoetropes

## Investigations

### I wonder whether ...

- **food colourings mix in the way paints do?**

For best effect, ensure that the water is still. Children make detailed observations, adding one drop of colour at a time. Predict what patterns will be made when the colours are dropped in different combinations. Predict what colour will appear when the water is stirred.

Discuss the best way of recording observations; this may provide a link with art, creative writing, or graphics on the computer.

- **a red tomato always looks red?**

Look at a yellow pencil and a green plant through a green plastic bottle.

Make a secret message.

Find a jumper or a book in which the pattern or the letters disappear when looked at through a transparent object of a particular colour.

Observe and record.

**• hollow dish-shaped mirrors give a different image from mirrors which bulge out like a ball?**

Children observe and draw the image of the same simple object seen in differently shaped mirrors.

Children 'catch' the image from a good quality shaving mirror on a card, and observe that it is upside-down and reversed.

**• I can find something which magnifies as well as a lens?**

Fill a clear plastic bottle with water, screw the lid on tightly and dry it. Look at words or pictures through its sides.

A shallow dish made by cutting the base from a two-litre lemonade bottle should have six sections. By moving a little water around from section to section, children could investigate whether a large drop of water magnifies better than a small one.

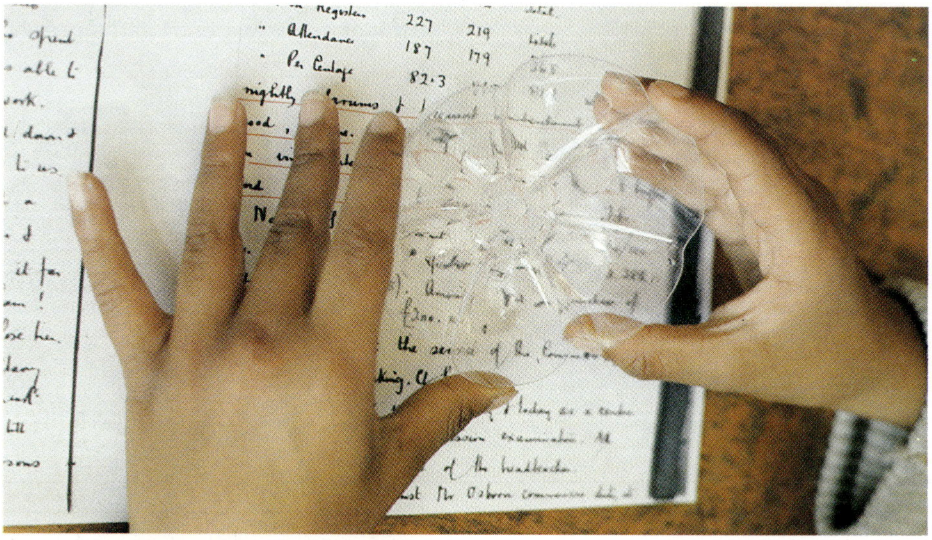

Take a laminated workcard, place a single drop of water over a letter and observe. Add more drops to find out which shape of drop makes the best magnifier. Record by drawing.

- **everybody holds a magnifying glass the same distance from the object being observed?**

Make the investigation fair by making sure each child's head is at the same level. Design an experiment with due regard to safety: for example, with no possibility of a ruler in the eye!

## What happens if ...

- **we turn on a torch in a dark box?**

Place a well known object in the box, and make predictions. Hypothesise that without light, we cannot see.

Can living things exist where there is no light? What might they look like? What do they look like?

- **we place objects in a torch beam?**

Observe shadow shape and quality depending on the nearness of the object to the light source.

- Which objects stop the light completely (opaque)?
- Which objects let a little light through (translucent)?
- Which objects don't seem to interfere with the light at all (transparent)?

- **we place a flat mirror in light rays?**

Make beams by shining a torch through a comb or through cardboard slits. Try changing the angle of the flat mirror.

Children observe and measure to find that the rays of light hitting a flat mirror bounce back at a matching angle. They may use this knowledge to explain how a periscope works.

- **we place a lens in light rays?**

Children find out which lens(es) will bring the light rays to a focus. They could think about the different uses of these lenses.

- **we change the order of ROYGBIV colours in a spinner?**

Children will observe that the colours merge. They could try to get as close as possible to white.

- **we try to copy a pattern which is reflected in a mirror?**

Set up two flat mirrors on stands. Pairs of children could compete to trace a path from A to B on a wiggly track, or draw round a shape. Design a way to stop them looking directly at their hands; they must look in the mirror!

Should the fastest or the most accurate win? Are timers and adjudicators needed? Set puzzles for other pairs. Does performance improve with practice?

## Can I find a way to …

- **make a dark area big enough to work in?**

Use a blacked-out storeroom, a table covered by a dark cloth which reaches to the ground, a play house, an igloo tent or a very large cardboard container. Experiment with different ways of blacking out windows.

- **send a message using light?**

Predict what would be the best 'shiny surface' (reflector) to use.

Plan a signalling system, and experiment to find out if it works. Can it be improved (on review)? When might someone need a system like this?

- **make a coloured shadow?**

Stand a small object in front of a white background. Shine torches covered in coloured cellophane individually, then in combination. Do the primary colours of light (red, blue and green) combine as paints of these colours do?

- **make a giant's shadow for our puppet play?**

Children can use jointed figures made for an 'Ourselves' investigation, or make an animal using their hands. Depending on the strength of the available light source, the children could discuss which material makes the best screen and how it should be supported so that the whole class can see.

Decide how to make the classroom darker if necessary to make the shadows clearer. Find out how to get the sharpest image and whether the giant character can be made using the same sized figure as the others.

- **work out whether a mirror, large enough to see ourselves from head to toe, will fit on the bedroom wall?**

Children work in pairs.

One child stands still in front of a large, wall-mounted mirror and guides the partner to stick a strip of masking tape where (s)he sees the top of the reflection's head and another where (s)he sees the toes. Measure the distance between the two, remembering to include the width of the tapes. Look for and record patterns across the class.

Can children then predict the result for someone not yet measured? (The mirror must be half the person's height.)

If this is done on a patterned floor, children may observe by counting the patterns that their image is as far 'behind' the mirror as they are in front of it.

**• make an advertisement which stands out from the others?**

Children should observe advertisements in magazines or on hoardings and discuss the features which 'caught their eye'. How important was colour?

The children could write advertisements for something they want to 'sell' on the classroom board. Have they done better than the adults?

**• make a rainbow?**

*Outside* Children using a prism will find that placing a sheet of white paper in some shade will help them see the colours more clearly. Slowly rotate the prism in full sunlight, and bring the rainbow (spectrum) on to the paper. Where do the colours come from?

*Inside* Make a 'sharp' beam of light by blacking out a window with newspaper, and sticking a piece of black paper over it. Cut a 1 cm slit and rotate the prism in this beam.

**• show that light is bent by some materials?**

Observe a pencil standing upright by a transparent baking dish, or sticking out from a beaker of water. The light is 'bent' by the glass and by water.

Place a penny in the bottom of an empty bowl. Children look at the penny over the rim and mark the level of their eye where they can just see it (use a ruler). They then move their heads to just below this point. A partner pours water into the bowl and the penny comes back into view. Emphasise the fact that the light between the penny and their eye is bent (refracted) by the water.

**Unit** ........................ **Date** ........................

# Teaching

**Have the children been provided with opportunities to:**

- work on questions or problems which they have accepted as their own? ☐
- develop their skills of exploration and investigation? ☐

See AT 1 evaluation checklist (page 11).

**Has the work pupils were engaged in allowed them to:**

PS 15
- explore the effect of light passing through:
  - lenses? ☐
  - colour filters? ☐
  - water? ☐
  - prisms? ☐
  - other transparent objects? ☐
- investigate:
  - shadows? ☐
  - images in flat mirrors? ☐
  - images in curved mirrors? ☐
  - images in other objects and devices? ☐
- record, by representing in drawings and diagrams, their ideas about how light behaves in terms of:
  - light? ☐
  - colour? ☐
  - shade? ☐

PS 13
- investigate the range of fuels (energy sources) used in their school, and their efficient and economical use? ☐

**Unit ......................** **Date ........................**

## Learning

**Using investigations based on this unit, have the children demonstrated that they:**

**Level 1**

**AT 15** • know that light comes from different sources? ☐

**Level 2**

**AT 15** • know that light passes through some materials and not others, and that when it does not, shadows may be formed? ☐

• can draw pictures showing features such as light, colour and shade? ☐

**Level 3**

AT 15 • know that light can be made to change direction? ☐

– and shiny surfaces can form images? ☐

• can give an account of an investigation with mirrors? ☐

AT 13 • understand, in qualitative terms, that models and machines need a source of energy in order to work? ☐

**Level 4**

AT 15 • know that we see objects because light is scattered off them and into our eyes? ☐

• know that light travels in straight lines? ☐

– and use this to explain the shapes and sizes of shadows? ☐

**Level 5**

AT 15 • understand how light is reflected? ☐

See AT 1 evaluation checklist (page 11).

# UNIT 2
# NOISE AND MUSIC

## Opportunities for learning

Working from this unit, children will be developing their investigative skills and their knowledge and understanding of:

- the properties, transmission and absorption of sound
- information transfer

For greater detail, refer to the evaluation checklist (teaching) at the end of this unit.

## Topics

| | |
|---|---|
| **CELEBRATIONS AROUND THE WORLD / FESTIVALS** | Instruments from other countries / cultures |
| **LEISURE** | Music, musicians |
| **HOW WE USED TO LIVE** | Ear trumpets, gramophones with horns<br>Morse Code, Crystal sets |
| **THE LOCAL ENVIRONMENT** | Pollution<br>Animal noises and their senses<br>Response to vibration |
| **PEOPLE WHO HELP US** | The emergency services, useful sounds, alarms |

## Cross-curricular links

| | |
|---|---|
| **ENGLISH** | Using tapes / records, stories with sound effects |
| **GEOGRAPHY** | Instruments and sounds linked with particular cultures (castanets, balalaika, sitar) |
| **HISTORY** | Ancient or 'early' music |
| **MATHEMATICS** | Measurement and shape |
| **TECHNOLOGY** | Making instruments |

## Classroom materials

The following *Nelson Science* materials support this unit:

**Picture Resource Book 1**

- p.2 – insect noises
- p.17 – the noise of a storm, or of trees falling

**Picture Resource Book 2**

- p.8 –18 – animal noises

**Picture Resource Book 3**

- p.1 - musicians
- p.2 - the vibration of a string
- p.3, 4 - noise pollution by machines

**Science Explorers**

- **Carrying Out Surveys 1, 2 and 3**
- **Experimenting 1, 2 and 3**
- **Problem Solving 1, 2 and 3**

## Related units

### Units in the Teacher's Classroom Manual (Key Stage 2)

- The local environment and beyond - Unit 4
- How animals work - Unit 8
- Everyday materials - Unit 13

### Units in the Teacher's Classroom Manual (Key Stage 1)

- Sounds - Unit 2

## Resources and equipment

- tuning forks
- a variety of elastic bands, pieces of wood, lengths of string, grades of sandpaper; plastic tubing, glue and woodworking tools (especially a hacksaw)
- clay flowerpots, foam pipe lagging, identical bottles in sets, bottles in series, plastic containers, all in different sizes
- objects for shakers and to demonstrate vibration, such as dried peas, small beads, sand or rice
- a variety of boxes in different sizes
- a selection of musical instruments: xylophone, tambourine, recorder, guitar, triangle, cymbal

### Safety

Ensure that the children:

- use mouthpieces which have been sterilised
- never put objects in their ears
- handle any small, loose objects over a tray; accidental spillage must be cleared up immediately to prevent falls
- take care when taking home small items in shakers; these can be dangerous for younger brothers and sisters
- take care when tensioning string or elastic, especially if using weights, and keep all parts of the body out of the way

## Starting points

### The school environment

- sound in the classroom:
– a working hum or unacceptable noise?
– noisy, echoing corridors or dining room
– fire drill
- music: school choir/ orchestra/ recorder group:
– items for the school talent show
– items to accompany the next class assembly
– songs for a particular time of year, religious festivals
– a visit to school by accomplished musicians
- medicals and hearing tests:
– a child in the class with a hearing aid

### The social environment

- children talking about:
– pop groups, discos
– warnings: shouts, alarm clocks, seeing and hearing emergency services at work, a pelican crossing
– frightening sounds in the night
– animal noises, talking birds
– noisy toys and computer games
– soundproofing (having seen advertisements for double glazing)
– unacceptable noise: pollution

### Further afield

- children visiting:
– a building with a 'whispering gallery' (for example, St Paul's Cathedral)
– a place which produces echoes, for example under bridges, in castles, on hillsides
– concerts
– a natural history museum
– the countryside

Also see 'Making connections'.

## Asking questions

**I wonder whether ...**

- **we can stop a sound quickly or make it go on for longer?**
- **sound can travel through anything other than air?**
- **we can identify each other's voices from a tape?**

## Gathering information

**Carrying out surveys**

**Collecting information about:**
- **vibrations - children use familiar objects which make a sound, and then find the quickest way(s) to stop it or make it last longer**
- **materials other than air which allow sound to pass through**
- **the timbre of voices - children speak into the tape recorder, and others try to guess which voice is which**

## Asking questions

### What happens if ...

- we cup our hands to our ears?
- we alter (vary) a plucked string?
- we make instruments especially to be plucked, scraped, shaken, struck or blown and then try to get a sound by another method?

### Can I find a way to ...

- 'see' the vibrations of a sound?
- 'feel' the vibrations of a sound?
- make a quiet corner in the classroom or stop the computer printer being so noisy?
- make noises so that another group can easily guess 'where I am now'?
- show that it takes time for sound to travel?

## Gathering information

### Experimenting

**Children:**

- progress from the discovery that sounds are made louder if they cup their hands to their ears, by finding other simple amplifiers
- investigate a string fixed at one end and then stretched over wood
- choose suitable materials for making instruments and are encouraged to think about which materials vibrate

### Solving practical problems

- To 'see' sound vibrations, children:
  - touch a 'sounding' tuning fork on a water surface
  - 'twang' a ruler held in a desk or a piece of wood clamped on a surface and observe
  - stretch string between two nails, pluck and observe
  - stretch material over a basin, place a small amount of sand or rice on this tight 'skin', strike and observe
  - put dried peas or beads on a drum skin, strike and observe
- To 'feel' sound vibrations, children:
  - gently place their fingers on their throats, talk and feel their vocal cords vibrate
  - hold, with outstretched hands, a well inflated balloon, and then speak and interrupt the sound waves a short distance from their mouths
- Sound insulation - children design an experiment which uses easily available surfaces or materials to find which deaden (absorb) the sound best
- Using a tape recorder, children create sounds to imitate different environments.
- To perceive that sound takes time to travel, children experience the time difference between seeing and hearing for example: aeroplanes, cars, someone striking a ball with a wooden bat

Examples of ways in which these ideas have been developed in the classroom are provided on pages 34–41.

## Handling information

- Encourage systematic listing and recording of data:
  - frequency tables

| Tuning Forks group two | |
|---|---|
| Objects Which Absorb Sound | Objects Which Make Sounds Continue |
| MY HANDS | PLASTIC BOX |
| A RAG | SHOE BOX |
| BOX FULL OF STUFFING | METAL BOX |
| CARPET | TABLE TOP |
| TENNIS BALL | TAMBOURINE |

  - bar charts
- Encourage searching for patterns in data.
- Encourage written and/or oral reporting skills as appropriate.

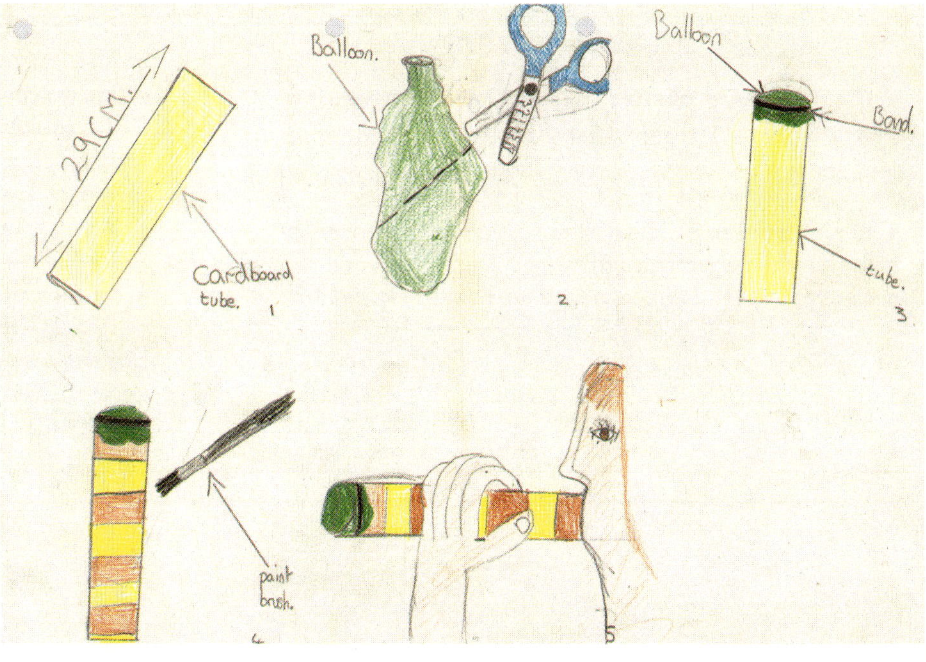

- Encourage the use of a limited technical vocabulary in communicating findings and ideas.
- Encourage the interpretation of data, and evaluation against the demands of the problem.

## Review points

The following are useful talking points:

### Our investigations

- new vocabulary we learned; for example: *vibration, timbre, absorb, amplitude, pitch;* can we add to our definitions?
- the questions we raised that we answered, and those we must leave unanswered
- the variables we controlled, and those we should have or would like to have controlled
- the new equipment we used, or skills we learned; were we successful? do we need more practice?
- any patterns we noticed in the data or tentative hypotheses we made

### Making connections

- using recorded sound: the faster the vibration the higher the sound; playing a familiar record too fast gives a squeaky voice, and playing it more slowly gives a deep, low voice
- noise pollution, obtrusive sounds
- useful sounds
- the fact that sound takes time to travel, deduced from observing lightning/echoes
- heat insulation compared with sound insulation

## Investigations

### I wonder whether ...

- **we can stop a sound quickly or make it go on for longer?**

Using commercially produced or home-made musical instruments, dampen the sound with the hand or another object, for example, a solid table, a wooden box or a tin.

Which objects: - make the sound last longer?
- amplify the sound?
- stop the sound?

- **sound can travel through anything other than air?**

Children draw on their own experience; they may have heard central heating pipes knocking or taken care of an aquarium.

Using a tuning fork (a very long pronged fork is a poor substitute), strike a note and listen to it after the fork has been banged on cork. Predict and record, then listen and record its sound in air, on wood (touch on solid wood and boxes), in water (in bottles, a jar, a bowl).

Use secondary sources to find out how animals such as whales or dolphins communicate through water.

- **we can identify each other's voices from a tape?**

Children in one group say a number first to identify themselves before recording the same sentence (fair testing). Children in another group match the names to the numbers. Reflect on how hard or easy the task was, and how we use the quality or timbre of the sound to identify individuals.

## What happens if ...

- **we cup our hands to our ears?**

Children investigate other ways to make a sound louder.

Other simple amplifiers can be made, for example:

– a sounding box; touch a tuning fork on to a box to compare it with a solid table

– a stethoscope made from a length of tube with a small funnel on the end

– an ear trumpet, using a long cardboard tube or simply a long piece of dowelling; try listening to a wristwatch with this

- **we alter (vary) a plucked string?**

Children stretch thin, waxed string from a nail in a wooden block across dowelling frets, then investigate the effect of changing the length and tension of the string, changing the thickness of the string and using another material. (Beware of elastic bands when increasing tension; they break very suddenly!) Encourage 'fair testing' throughout.

**• we make instruments especially to be plucked, scraped, shaken, struck or blown and then try to get a sound by another method?**

An instrument which makes a sound when plucked:

– Use experience of investigations in which the string on a block is varied, and combine with different sizes of sounding box, up to tea-chest size.

An instrument which makes a sound when scraped:

– Investigate using sanding blocks and different grades of sandpaper, washboards, and steel brushes on sanding boxes and other surfaces.

An instrument which makes a sound when shaken:

– Use a variety of containers, including papier-mâché 'balloons', tins, and delicatessen packaging tubs fastened in pairs.

– Use a variety of ‘fillings’ including peas, barley, pebbles and macaroni.

An instrument which makes a sound when struck:

– Investigate sets of bottles in series and with different amounts of water in them.

– Hang flowerpots in series from a frame.

– Hang metal tubes in a series from a frame (tubular bells).

– Experiment with a variety of materials stretched over containers (drum).

– Arrange bars of wood in series over supports insulated with foam pipe lagging to allow vibration (xylophone). Try striking them with mallets made from different materials.

An instrument which makes a sound when blown:

– Investigate straws with their tops made into 'vibrators'.

– Arrange bottles in series with different amounts of water in them.

– Try a swanee whistle.

– Connect a metre of rubber hosepipe to a funnel .

Can children make a high, a low, a loud and a soft sound using their instruments? Which sound(s) are made most easily? Which instrument makes the most pleasant sound?

### Can I find a way to ...

- **'see' the vibrations of a sound?**

Children will observe that the greater the distance the ruler moves through (the bigger the amplitude of the vibration), the louder the sound. Devise a fair test. Record results on a tape recorder or fasten a pen or crayon to the ruler to write on paper fixed to a wall.

Vary the length of the ruler, to make the sound become higher or lower (a change of pitch).

Much more attractive sounds can be made in investigating other materials which can be plucked (the timbre improves).

- **'feel' the vibrations of a sound?**

- **make a quiet corner?**

– Build on children's experiences of dampening sound.

– Go on a 'sound walk', noting and recording how sounds vary in the context of different wall surfaces. Devise a fair test to determine the most appropriate materials. Remember to think about cost.

– Using secondary sources children could research other methods of cutting noise – for example, double glazing or blinds.

– Use really large boxes (for example, from an electrical goods retailer) to make telephone booths. How do they improve the performance of string telephones?

- **make noises so that another group can easily guess 'where I am now'?**

Children could imitate 'kitchen' sounds: sizzle, bang, scratch, scrape, grate, knock, drip, whoosh, whirr.

They could develop their ideas into sound effects to accompany an adventure story or a poem, or into discussions about loud and soft noises, angry and happy noises, funny and sad noises, frightening and comforting noises.

- **show that it takes time for sound to travel?**

Estimating or using digital watches, children could try the following:

– Using blindfolds, see whether the children can match the sound of an aeroplane with its position (it is seen before it is heard).

– Send a pair of children with a wooden bat and a ball as far away as possible on a still day. They see the ball hit before they hear the click.

– Experiment with echoes; measure the time taken to hear the sound bounced back.

# Evaluation Checklist

**Unit ......................** **Date ......................**

## Teaching

**Have the children been provided with opportunities to:**

- work on questions or problems which they have accepted as their own? ☐
- develop their skills of exploration and investigation? ☐

See AT 1 evaluation checklist (page 11).

**Has the work pupils were engaged in allowed them to:**

PS 14
- become aware of the way sound is heard and the fact that sounds, including musical notes, are made in a variety of ways, and can be pleasant or obtrusive in the environment? ☐
- explore changes in:
  - – pitch? ☐
  - – loudness? ☐
  - – timbre of a sound? ☐
- ... by changing the:
  - – length? ☐
  - – tension? ☐
  - – thickness? ☐
  - – material of a vibrating object? ☐
- ... and through different ways of causing the sound, for example:
  - – using different mallets? ☐
  - – overblowing? ☐

PS12
- use and investigate the transmission of information using the telephone? ☐
- use tape recorders in experiments and to store, retrieve and present their work? ☐

PHOTOCOPY

**Unit..........................** **Date.........................**

# Learning

**Using investigations based on this unit, have the children demonstrated that they:**

**Level 1**

**AT 14** • know that sounds can be made in a variety of ways? ☐

**Level 2**

**AT 14** • know that sounds are heard when the sound reaches the ear? ☐

• (can) explain how musical sounds are produced in simple musical instruments? ☐

**Level 3**

AT 14 • know that sounds are produced by vibrating objects? ☐

– and can travel through different materials? ☐

• (can) give a simple explanation of the way in which sound is generated? ☐

– and can travel through different materials? ☐

AT 12 • (can) store information using devices, for example, a tape recorder? ☐

**Level 4**

AT 14 • know that it takes time for sound to travel? ☐

AT 12 • know about the range and uses of microelectronic devices in everyday life? ☐

**Level 5**

AT 14 • understand that the frequency of a vibrating source affects the pitch of the sound it produces? ☐

• understand the relationship between the loudness of the sound and the amplitude of vibration of the source? ☐

• understand the importance of noise control in the environment? ☐

AT 5 • (can) describe the sources, implications and possible prevention of pollution? ☐

See AT 1 evaluation checklist (page 11).

# UNIT 3
# CIRCUITS, SWITCHING AND CONTROL

## Opportunities for learning

Working from this unit, children will be developing their investigative skills and their knowledge and understanding of:

- electric and electromagnetic effects in simple circuits, electrical devices, domestic appliances and microelectronics

For greater detail, refer to the evaluation checklist (teaching) at the end of this unit.

## Topics

| | |
|---|---|
| COMMUNICATION | Business and household emergency services |
| HOMES AND BUILDINGS | Energy: storage, saving and supply |

## Cross-curricular links

| | |
|---|---|
| GEOGRAPHY | The availability of electricity or other means of communication in different societies; are they truly essential?<br>Drawing / diagrams in map work and cross-sectional representations |
| HISTORY | Volta, Leclanche, Samuel Morse<br>Life before electricity |
| TECHNOLOGY | Energy sources control |

## Classroom materials

The following *Nelson Science* materials support this unit:

**Picture Resource Book 1**

- p.3 – traffic lights, street lights
- p.6 – a miner's safety hat
- p.20 – always match the voltage written on the battery with that written on the bulbs to make sure we do not 'blow' the bulbs
  – note which are the positive and negative terminals when connecting batteries
- p.21 – electricity pylons and sub-stations
- p.22 – switching and microelectronic control of electrical appliances in the kitchen

**Science Explorers**

- **Carrying Out Surveys 1, 2 and 3**
- **Experimenting 1, 2 and 3**
- **Problem Solving 1, 2 and 3**

## Related units

### Units in the Teacher's Classroom Manual (Key Stage 2)

- Colour, mirrors, lenses and prisms - Unit 1
- Noise and music - Unit 2
- The local environment and beyond - Unit 4
- Measuring the weather - Unit 9
- Movement, forces and energy - Unit 11
- Everyday materials - Unit 13

### Units in the Teacher's Classroom Manual (Key Stage 1)

- How to make bulbs light and buzzers sound - Unit 3

## Resources and equipment

- bulbs (1.5 v or 2.5 v) for general use, plus a collection of bulbs up to 6 volts to show different shapes and voltages for different purposes
- batteries to match 'classroom use' bulbs, plus a collection of all shapes and sizes

  If commercially produced battery and bulb holders are used, screwdrivers are needed and the voltage of the batteries must be matched to the voltage of the bulbs.
- plastic film containers or other means of storage
- plastic-coated wire (especially single-strand rather than multi-strand), bare wire and waxed wire
- wire strippers and cutters
- aluminium foil, aluminium take-away containers, paperclips, drawing pins, nails, polystyrene, pipe cleaners, steel wool, elastic bands, clothes pegs, corks, metal strips from packing cases
- small (6 cm by 4 cm) pieces of soft board as firm bases for switches
- 'junk' materials for model making
- plotting compasses, `field' compasses
- magnets
- crocodile clips (not essential)
- small electric motors
- small cardboard boxes (such as shoe boxes), each of which will store one group's basic kit

## Safety

Ensure that the children:

- take care with mains electricity; warnings need repeating
- take care with wire strippers and cutters; demonstrate their safe use
- use batteries which are in good condition; check for leakage as the contents of batteries may be corrosive or poisonous

## Starting points

### The school environment

- a power cut (real or imagined)
- instruments and equipment used by the children, for example, tape recorder, calculators, computers, light or heat sensors
- models which could be fitted with flashing lights, burglar alarms, vehicles which could be `powered'
- battery-operated toys

### The social environment

- shopping: automatic car park barriers, supermarket check-outs, bar codes
- children's conversations about items which use electricity: television, computer games, video, digital watches, cars, traffic lights, electronic keyboards, answering machines, burglar alarms, bicycle lamps
- electricians in the home, for example to re-wire
- wiring plans
- lights for special occasions, for example the Blackpool Illuminations or *Son et Lumière* performances

### Further afield

- electricity pylons
- visits to a power station, a lighthouse, a telephone exchange, emergency service control stations, a local radio station, a television studio
- visits to museums

Also see 'Making connections'.

## Asking questions

### I wonder whether ...

- **any other material is as good as wire in conducting electricity to light a bulb?**
- **every bulb has a filament?**
- **the bigger the battery, the more power it has?**
- **there is a quick way of recording electrical circuits?**

## Gathering information

### Carrying out surveys

**Children:**

- **construct a circuit to find the best substitute materials to complete the circuit and make the bulb light; they use their previous experience of conductivity**
- **observe a range of electric bulbs; using a hand lens they can become familiar with their construction and the symbols on the metal collar**
- **use or simply handle a range of batteries (for example 1.5 v), then look on the cases to note the voltage; how many battery shapes can they collect?**
- **find out about the symbols used in drawing electrical circuits**

## Asking questions

### What happens if ...

- I connect light bulbs in a long string?
- I connect light bulbs in parallel?
- I put a compass needle near a wire carrying electricity?
- I put a very thin strand of wire in a circuit?
- I put two switches in a circuit?

### Can I find a way to ...

- make a bulb tester using only one wire?
- make a light bulb holder?
- stop the battery rolling off the desk?
- make a switch?
- make a switch to make lights flash or a dimmer switch?
- make a circuit which would work my model traffic lights?
- find a faulty wire?
- make a light-up quiz board?
- make my 'buggy' go?

## Gathering information

### Experimenting

Children:

- connect at least two bulbs in a line (in series) and observe the effects, especially the brightness of the bulbs, if one bulb is disconnected
- connect at least two bulbs in parallel and observe the effects, especially the brightness of the bulbs, if one bulb is disconnected
- form 30 coils of wire round a pencil; when a plotting compass is brought near to it, the needle will be deflected
  How does this compare to the deflections caused by a bar magnet?
- use a strand from a pad of steel wool after observing bulb filaments so they understand the need for caution
- predict, experiment and record their results using simple home-made on/off switches; where might different circuits be useful?

### Solving practical problems

- Children must understand the construction of the bulb to get it to light.
- The understanding from the above exercise is invaluable in constructing a bulb holder. Polystyrene, corks or pegs are favourite 'bases'.
- Ideas could range from a looped piece of masking tape, 'sitting' in a cradle made from foam lagging, to a more elaborate wood and clip battery holder.
- Starting with basic on/off switches or pressure switches, the notion of a switch as a controllable way of breaking a circuit may be conveyed. Children can then be very inventive.
- 'Specialist' switches can be 'cued' by stories or scenarios explaining the need, for example, theatre lights, or television brightness control.
- More OR and AND gates (see above)
- Use a bundle of identical wires, the deliberate fault hidden under tape, or inside a box.
- Children may reflect that the 'fault-finding' challenge may be adapted to a quiz board which lights up when you have the right answer.

Examples of ways in which these ideas have been developed in the classroom are provided on pages 50–55.

## Handling information

- Encourage systematic listing and recording of data:
  - frequency tables

  - bar charts
- Encourage searching for patterns in data.
- Encourage written and/or oral reporting skills as appropriate.

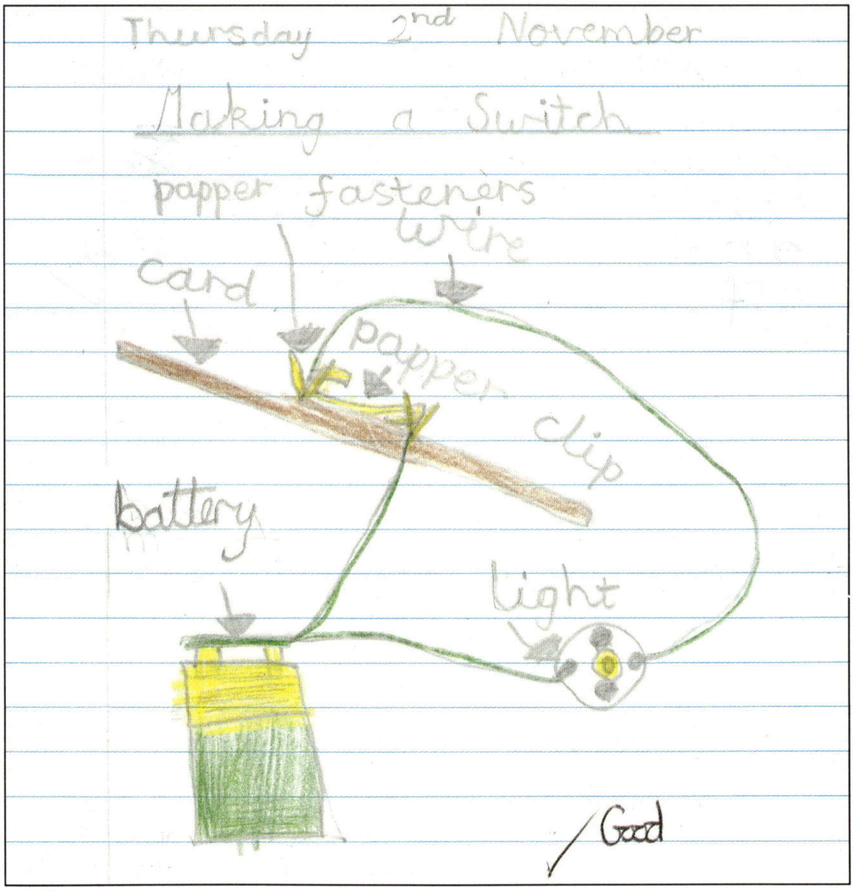

- Encourage the use of a limited technical vocabulary in communicating findings and ideas.

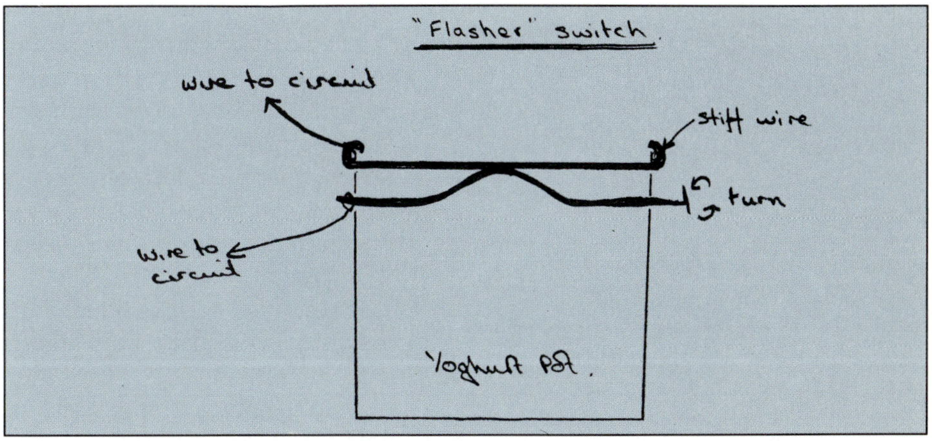


- Encourage the interpretation of data, and evaluation against the demands of the problem.

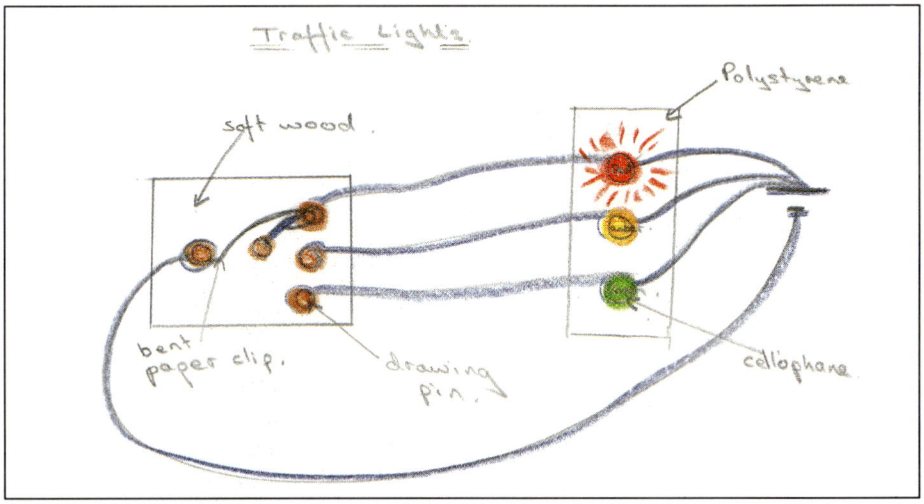


## Review points

The following are useful talking points:

### Our investigations

- new vocabulary we learned; for example: *instrument, circuit, switch, battery, terminals, positive, negative, bulb, screwdriver, connect, contact, microelectronics, digital, information, communication, programmable, select, retrieve, store, conduct, conductor, insulate, insulator, symbol, series, parallel, volts, voltage, compass, generator, dynamo, pylon;* can we add to our definitions?
- the questions we raised that we answered, and those we must leave unanswered
- the variables we controlled, and those we should have or would like to have controlled
- the new equipment we used, or skills we learned; were we successful? do we need more practice?
- any patterns we noticed in the data or tentative hypotheses we made

## Making connections

- water as a conductor of electricity and the need for a pull-cord in the bathroom
- safety clothing worn by workers in the electricity industry
- the National Grid and the massive voltage transmitted on overhead cables; compare to 240 v (domestic voltage which can kill), and a torch battery (6 v)
- action to take (and not to take) if children find someone who has received an electric shock; turn off the supply if possible, and never touch the person
- microelectronic devices in everyday life, for example, programmable washing machines, record/ cassette players, videos, microwave ovens, CD players
- electromagnets in breakers' yards, telephones
- the fact that electrical appliances get warm after they have been left on for some time
- bicycle dynamos (generators) show how electricity may be generated to light a bulb

## Investigations

### I wonder whether ...

**• any other material is as good as wire in conducting electricity to light a bulb?**

The children could make predictions; emphasise the fact that a continuous metal circuit is needed. Children could work out their own criteria for 'best', for example, cheapest, bendiest, least likely to tear.

**• every bulb has a filament?**

A trip to a high street chain store known for car and bicycle accessories will produce a variety of 2.4 v bulbs with different ampage (or brightness). Warn children against looking directly at a 6 v bulb lit by a 6 v battery, as this will hurt their eyes. (Never look at anything brighter.) However, a 6 v bulb lit by a 1.5 v battery will make the filament glow enough if a 'cue' for this investigation is required.

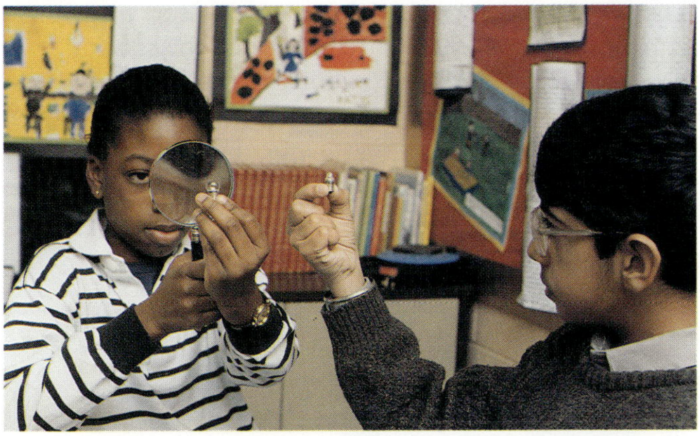

- **the bigger the battery, the more power it has?**

Using the same circuit and a 2.5 v bulb, children could predict which shape of 1.5 v battery will make the bulb brightest.

- **there is a quick way of recording electrical circuits?**

Drawing 'pictures' can be a very time-consuming method of recording when there are only slight changes to the circuit. Children could make up their own system, and then compare it to 'officially agreed' ones to help them understand the need for a 'universal language' in electrical symbols.

### What happens if ...

- **I connect light bulbs in a long string?**

This is traditionally one of the first activities following the 'simple circuit'. Check that the bulbs are the same voltage and ampage, and preferably from the same 'batch' as differences in brightness can cause frustration and / or erroneous ideas.

- **I connect light bulbs in parallel?**

This is often a good opportunity to talk about avoiding 'short circuits' which run the batteries flat. Circuits should only be kept joined up while children are testing their ideas, and then immediately disconnected.

For children who don't understand the terminology, a drawing or even joining hands within the group may help.

- **I put a compass needle near a wire carrying electricity?**

Children need to revise their Key Stage 1 experience of magnetism and compass needles. Plotting compasses are easily the most sensitive if these are available. If a soft iron rod is available, this could be placed in the space left by the pencil to give a stronger effect. The children could reflect on the uses for an 'electromagnet' or something which is a magnet only while the current is on.

Children could try winding 30-50 coils of waxed or cotton-covered wire round their hands. A compass placed in the centre of this coil will show a strong deflection when the circuit is complete. Reversing the battery will reverse the direction of the deflection. This is the principle behind a battery or circuit tester.

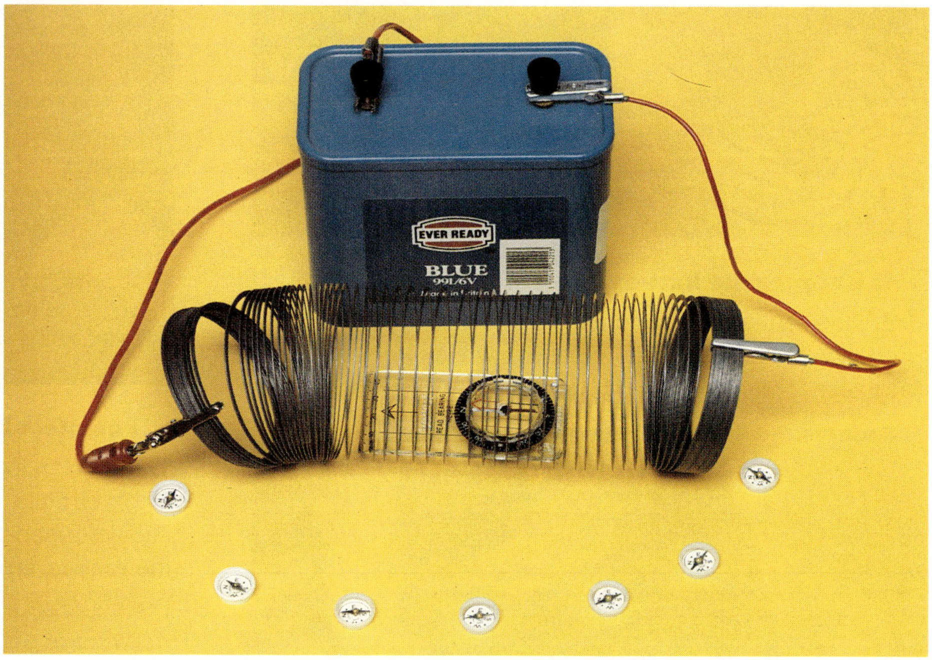


- **I put a very thin strand of wire in a circuit?**

This investigation could lead to a consideration of the need to use the right fuses for the protection of expensive electrical circuits.

- **I put two switches in a circuit?**

Children may connect them:

- in parallel, making a 'two-way' switch like a domestic light switch; note that this circuit is an OR gate.

- in series, making a circuit where both switches must be 'on' for the current to flow; this kind of circuit is used for safety, for example in a washing machine where the door must be closed and the socket switched on for it to work. Note that this circuit is an AND gate.

## Can I find a way to ...

- **make a bulb tester using only one wire?**

- **make a light bulb holder?**

A simple example is based on a polystyrene 'sandwich' with foil as the 'filling', held together with elastic bands. The upper 'slice' needs a hole in the centre to take the bulb. One wire is attached to the side of the bulb; tape the other to the foil.

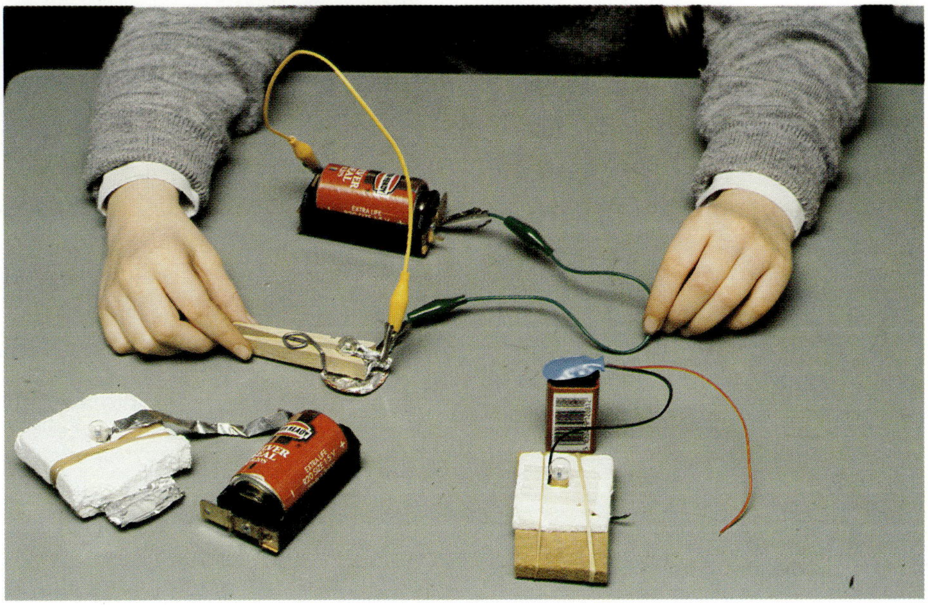

- **stop the battery rolling off the desk?**

This challenge is invaluable even if 'proper' battery holders are available as it helps with fault finding and evaluation of ideas.

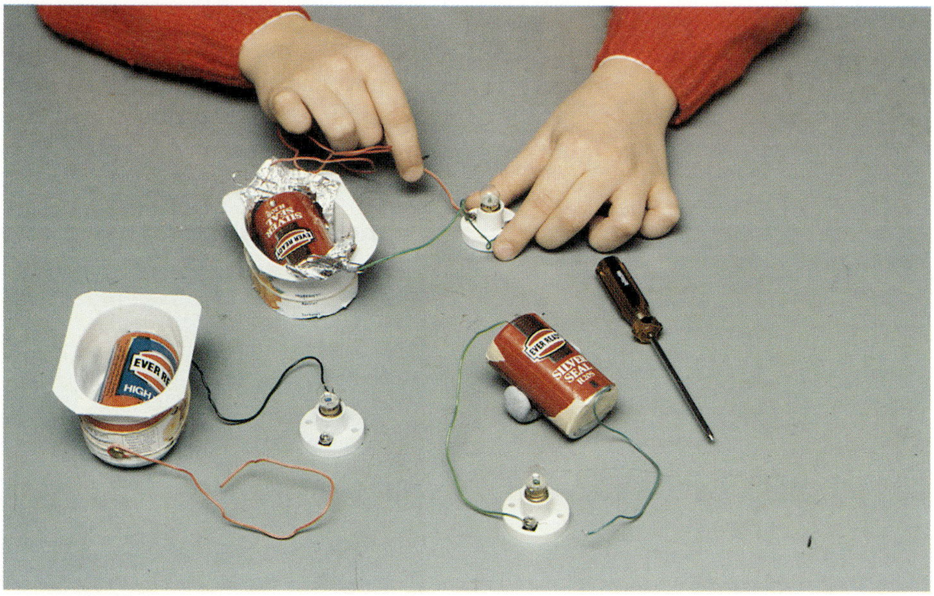

- **make a switch?**

*On/off switch*

Attach wires to two butterfly clips, brass paper fasteners or split pins set close together in a card. Connect using a paperclip.

Press two drawing pins into a soft wood base and connect with a paperclip or foil strip.

*Pressure switch*

Attach wires to two butterfly clips set close together in a card. Fold the card in two so that the butterfly clips touch.

Two foil 'plates' may be kept apart by a thin foam pad.

- **make a switch to make lights flash or a dimmer switch?**

To make a flashing control: using a straight wire for one battery connection across a yoghurt pot, bend stiff wire into a crank set to touch the first wire as it turns.

- **make a circuit which would work my model traffic lights?**

Using three bulbs (with wires attached) pressed through a polystyrene and foil sandwich (similar to the vertical bulb holder outlined above), design and make a switching system using drawing pins or butterfly clips connected to the bulbs, and a paperclip connector.

- **find a faulty wire?**

With a known 'good' battery and a known 'good' bulb, children systematically record until they find the faulty wire.

- **make a light-up quiz board?**

Provided that a way of keeping the circuit hidden is found, it is possible to devise a quiz board which will light up when the right answer is chosen.

- **make my 'buggy' go?**

The buggy must be sturdy enough to carry the weight of the battery and the motor. This takes a good deal of planning, and then comes the challenge of getting it to go straight!

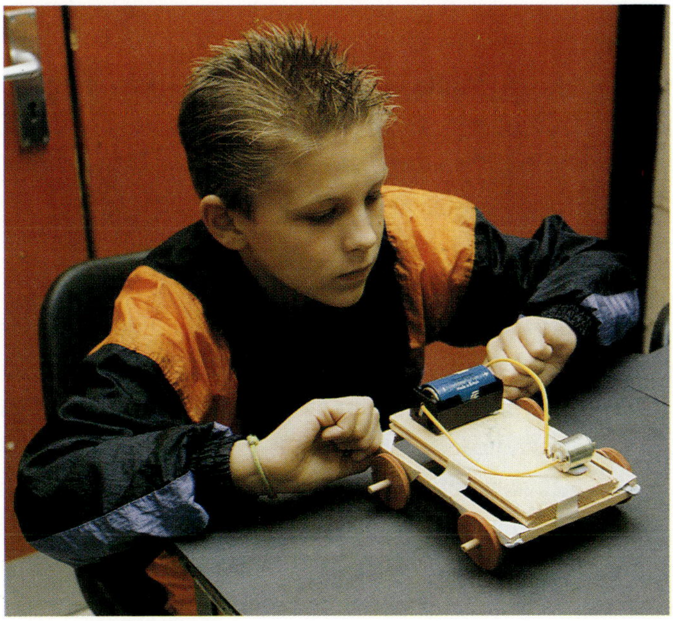

# Evaluation Checklist

**Unit ........................** **Date ........................**

## Teaching

**Have the children been provided with opportunities to:**

- work on questions or problems which they have accepted as their own?
- develop their skills of exploration and investigation?

See AT 1 evaluation checklist (page 11).

**Has the work pupils were engaged in allowed them to:**

PS 11
- construct simple circuits and investigate:
  - the effects of using different components?
  - the effects of varying the flow of electricity?
  - heating effects?
  - magnetic effects?
- learn how to record the construction details of a circuit by drawings and diagrams?
- learn about dangers associated with mains electricity through research using secondary sources?
- investigate the properties of magnetic and non-magnetic materials?
- begin to investigate simple electronic circuits for:
  - measuring?
  - switching?
  - control?

PS12
- construct circuits which illustrate AND or NOT gates?

**Unit ......................** **Date ......................**

## Learning

**Using investigations based on this unit, have the children demonstrated that they:**

**Level 2**

AT 11
- know that magnets attract certain materials but not others and can repel each other? ☐
- understand the danger associated with the use of electricity, and know appropriate safety measures? ☐

**Level 3**

AT 11
- know that some materials conduct electricity well while others do not? ☐
- understand that a complete circuit is needed for an electrical device, such as a bulb or buzzer, to work? ☐

AT 13
- (can) use simple power sources (electric motors, rubber bands)? ☐
  – and devices which transfer energy (gears, belts, levers)? ☐

**Level 4**

AT 11
- (can) construct simple electrical circuits? ☐

AT 13
- understand that energy can be stored, and transferred to and from moving things? ☐

**Level 5**

AT 11
- (can) describe and record diagrammatically simple electrical circuits that they have made? ☐
- (can) vary the flow of electricity in a simple circuit and observe the effects? ☐

AT 12
- understand the function of switches and relays in simple circuits? ☐
  – (can) use switches and relays in simple circuits? ☐
- understand logic gates and their use in decision making and simple control circuits? ☐

See AT 1 evaluation checklist (page 11).

# UNIT 4
# THE LOCAL ENVIRONMENT AND BEYOND

## Opportunities for learning

Working from this unit, children will be developing their investigative skills and their knowledge and understanding of:

- the ways in which human activities affect the Earth, the range of energy sources and the issues involved in their exploitation

For greater detail, refer to the evaluation checklist (teaching) at the end of this unit. The checklist is particularly important for this unit, because the Programme of Study requires fieldwork which needs to be taken into account when planning.

## Topics

| |
|---|
| **THE ENVIRONMENT** |
| **POLLUTION** |

## Cross-curricular links

| | |
|---|---|
| **ENGLISH** | Debating a balanced view on issues frequently in the media<br>Planning and organising visits by writing letters and issuing invitations |
| **GEOGRAPHY** | Renewable and non-renewable resources<br>Pollution<br>Population growth<br>The effects on the environment of extracting natural resources<br>Activities which improve the local environment |
| **HISTORY** | The introduction of smokeless fuel<br>Smog |
| **TECHNOLOGY** | Projects on changing or improving the local environment |

## Classroom materials

The following *Nelson Science* materials support this unit:

**Picture Resource Book 1**

- p.8 - the (disappearing) oak tree and its associations with England
- p.4, 5, 10, 12, 13, 14, 20, 21, 22 – compared as hospitable environments

**Picture Resource Book 2**

- p.19 – treating a polluted bird
- p.20 – the challenge posed by waste
- p.21 – stages of decomposition in an apple

**Picture Resource Book 3**

- p.1 – buskers, sound in the environment
- p.3 – the urban environment
- p.4, 17 – agriculture (Whitemoor, Cornwall)
- p.5 – clay quarrying, showing its effect on the landscape
- p.14 – industrial pollution (Hebden Bridge, Yorkshire)
- p.19 – open-cast mining of iron ore (Libya)
- p.21 – electricity pylons and the environment

**Science Explorers**

- **Carrying Out Surveys 1, 2 and 3**
- **Experimenting 1, 2 and 3**
- **Problem Solving 1, 2 and 3**

## Related units

### Units in the Teacher's Classroom Manual (Key Stage 2)

All units have starting points which are firmly based on the environment of the child. The units below will be particularly useful in the context of Unit 4:

- Our bodies – Unit 5
- Living things in the local environment – Unit 7
- Measuring the weather – Unit 9
- Weathering, minerals, rocks and soil – Unit 12

### Units in the Teacher's Classroom Manual (Key Stage 1)

- Improving the appearance of the local environment – Unit 4

## Resources and equipment

- containers which can be used and disposed of
- washing-up liquid or other detergent
- birds' feathers
- funnels and beakers, or plastic squash bottles cut to give funnels and beakers
- a variety of grades of paper and something to draw circles with (filter paper is ideal, but not essential)
- yoghurt pots
- peat and sand
- a pond or other 'dirty' water, clean water, food colouring
- pipettes or water droppers
- card, foil, cotton thread, old tights, elastic bands
- trays, newspapers and rags for clearing up!
- plastic (disposable) gloves

## Safety

Ensure that the children:

- take care with waste disposal experiments from the point of view of what is being dumped (for example, sharp-edged glass or tin) and where it is dumped so as not to cause a nuisance or danger to others
- work under strict supervision when using fire; small quantities should be burned and children should be aware of the dangers of noxious fumes
- only cut plastic bottles themselves if they know how to do so safely
- do not use pond or canal water unless you have checked for safety; it may be contaminated with Weil's disease or infested seasonally by blue/green algae

## Starting points

### The school environment

- a project to help improve the local environment
- waste paper collections for school funds, or litter in the grounds
- dilemmas such as one class trying to attract a variety of birds with varied eating habits, and another class wanting to keep them away from plants they are growing
- videos on international problems, such as rain-forest decimation, the Loire valley dam, the 'pros' and 'cons' of nuclear power
- letters to national organisations such as the Countryside Commission, the Worldwide Fund for Nature, the National Trust, Greenpeace, Friends of the Earth, the Royal Society for the Protection of Birds
- a regularly updated collection of press cuttings about pollution, from the 'official' dumping of sludge in the North Sea to spectacular disasters such as oil spills
- counting the cost of leaving doors open in winter; learning to read gas or electricity meters, graphing consumption and making comparisons with in-school and out-of-school periods or winter and summer

### The social environment

- local planning developments
- local efforts to clean up canals and streams
- television reports from programmes such as 'Newsround'
- the global 'One World' response by the Red Cross and other organisations to emergencies caused by major disasters
- bottle banks, aluminium can and newspaper collections
- the need to clean windows, cars, buildings and road signs

### Further afield

- visits to farms, sewage disposal plants, mines, quarries, nuclear power stations
- EEC regulations for clean beaches

Also see 'Making connections'.

## Asking questions

### I wonder whether ...

- we can prevent pollution?
- we can estimate the amount of water used by the class in a week?
- dirty water can be cleaned?
- we could manage without electricity?
- all houses have the same sized windows?

### What happens if ...

- oil gets on a bird's feathers?

### Can I find a way to ...

- clean up oil spilled on a water surface?
- dispose of different waste materials?

## Gathering information

### Carrying out surveys

**Children:**

- 'brainstorm' on to sheets of paper in groups, on what pollution is and where it comes from
- gather information on the importance of water and all the ways in which their families use water; this can be related to work on conditions for plant growth or care of pets
- look at ways of cleaning water; their ideas on sieving or grading particles of soil [Unit 12] may lead to the notion of finer and finer 'sieves' and thus to the filtration of water
- 'brainstorm' on those 'essentials' of life which work by electricity
- look at variety in window design, especially in very cold and very hot countries

### Experimenting

**Children:**

- observe and record the appearance, texture and waterproofing of two similar feathers before dropping oil on to one of them

Make predictions, and then compare the two feathers after trying to clean the oil off with detergent.

### Solving practical problems

**Children:**

- observe that oil floats on the water surface, which poses special problems

Using secondary sources, find out how rescue workers clean vast tracts of sea. Simulate these methods in the classroom.

- choose suitable materials for investigations which include burying, burning and dumping of waste

Examples of ways in which these ideas have been developed in the classroom are provided on pages 63–67.

## Handling information

- Encourage systematic listing and recording of data:
  - frequency tables
  - bar charts
- Encourage searching for patterns in data.
- Encourage written and/or oral reporting skills as appropriate.

- Encourage the use of a limited technical vocabulary in communicating findings and ideas.

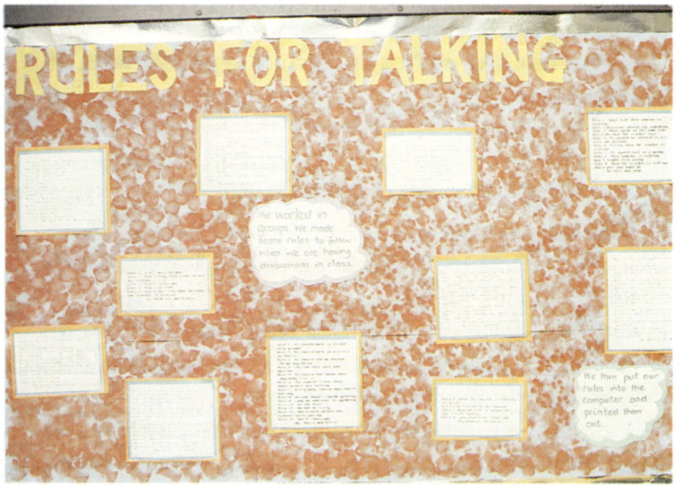


- Encourage the interpretation of data, and evaluation against the demands of the problem.

## Review points

The following are useful talking points:

### Our investigations

- new vocabulary we learned; for example: *pollution, pollutant, waste, litter, ecosystem, biodegradable, non-biodegradable, decay, life cycle, solvent, detergent, environment, locality, supply, recycling, flammable, inflammable, non-flammable, toxic, sewage, famine, consumer, consumption, producer, conservation, development, surface, impact, oil, effluent;* can we add to our definitions?
- the questions we raised that we answered, and those we must leave unanswered
- the variables we controlled, and those we should have or would like to have controlled
- the new equipment we used, or skills we learned; were we successful? do we need more practice?
- any patterns we noticed in the data or tentative hypotheses we made

### Making connections

'The environment' in its broadest sense is likely to be a major social, political and economic concern of future generations. It is hoped that teachers will enhance children's awareness of the challenge facing them whenever appropriate. As with multi-cultural and gender issues, environmental issues are important in terms of quality of life for everyone.

## Investigations

### I wonder whether ...

- **we can prevent pollution?**

After information from all the groups has been gathered and discussed, children discuss or list ideas about 'preventable pollution' and begin to face some of the issues.

- **we can estimate the amount of water used by the class in a week?**

In groups, children could work out appropriate means of estimating volume. For example, they could use washing-up bowls, baths and buckets as units of measurement. For water used in showers or hosepipes they could devise a way of estimating the amount of water flowing over a fixed period of time.

• **dirty water can be cleaned?**

Funnel and beaker sets can be made (in advance) from plastic squash bottles.

'Filter paper' may be made from a variety of different grades of paper, once children have worked out the size of circle required and the method of folding. (Fold circles into quarters, open out with three thicknesses on one side and one on the other, and pop the cone into the funnel.)

Pour some dirty water into the filter and observe.

Children could reflect on the impossibility of doing this for large quantities, such as those which reach the sewage works.

Make a 'filter bed' by placing layers of sand in a yoghurt pot (or similar) which has holes in the bottom. Dirty water poured in at the top will run out clear.

Try coloured water and include a layer of peat.

- **we could manage without electricity?**

How important is this energy source in our lives?

Where does it come from?

What can we substitute?

Do other energy sources have advantages or disadvantages when compared to electricity?

This investigation could be extended to a consideration of:

– global energy resources; these are limited and thus there is a need for fuel economy and efficiency

– 'alternative' technology

- **all houses have the same sized windows?**

This investigation provides an ideal vehicle for considering conflicting needs in terms of light, darkness, heat and coolness.

Children could think about the north- or south-facing aspects of their homes or the school, to link with work on energy efficiency and thermal insulation.

## What happens if …

- **oil gets on a bird's feathers?**

Children could devise ways of cleaning the oil off again, for example, using a standard household detergent (washing-up liquid).

Keep the untouched feather for comparison (the control). Observe and record the effect of a single drop of water on each, using a pipette. What has happened to the waterproofing and the way the barbs 'mend'?

What are the implications of this cleaning for oil-polluted birds or other creatures? Find out about the methods used by the RSPB to clean and rehabilitate birds.

Children may reflect on the problems facing other creatures when confronted by oil pollution.

This investigation may be extended to consider the risk of pollution at the point of production, and the transportation and use of all fuels.

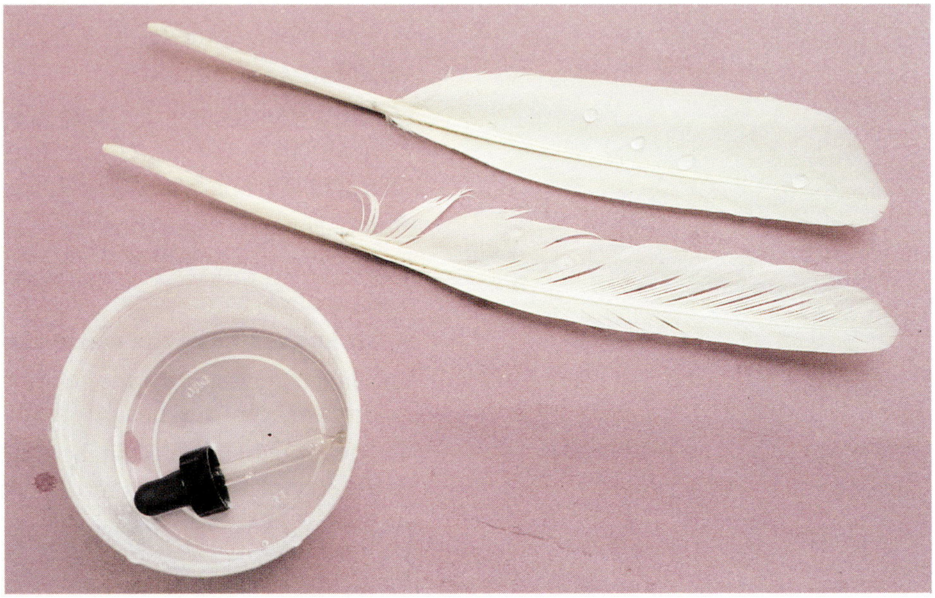

### Can I find a way to ...

- **clean up oil spilled on a water surface?**

This could be linked to the above investigation on cleaning dirty water.

Examples of cleaning methods include adding detergents and stirring, adding only the foam, 'bombing' with sand so that the oil sinks, and adding straw to absorb the pollutant.

Which is the best solution? Do all the containers have to be disposed of after this experiment?

- **dispose of different waste materials?**

How and where is waste of various kinds disposed of? Make a fair test for the effectiveness of burying, burning and dumping waste. For example, the air pollution caused by burning can be 'caught' using Vaseline-smeared saucers.

Design a record sheet to record the results over a period of time.

Is it possible to simulate all the methods of disposal, given your particular circumstances?

This investigation could be extended to a consideration of recycling. Children could try making paper.

# Evaluation Checklist

**Unit ......................** **Date ......................**

## Teaching

**Have the children been provided with opportunities to:**

- work on questions or problems which they have accepted as their own? ☐
- develop their skills of exploration and investigation? ☐

See AT 1 evaluation checklist (page 11).

**Has the work pupils were engaged in allowed them to:**

PS 5
- study aspects of their local environment which have been affected by human activity (for example, farming, industry, sewage disposal, mining or quarrying):
  - – through first-hand observation? ☐
  - – or through secondary sources where there are considerations of safety? ☐
- observe and record the significant features of the process, the range and origins of raw materials and the usefulness of any product(s) in:
  - – waste disposal procedures? ☐
  - – decay processes? ☐

PS 6
- learn about the dangers associated with the use of everyday materials such as bleach and hot oil? ☐

PS 13
- through first-hand methods and secondary sources, investigate the range of fuels (energy sources) used in their home or school, in terms of:
  - – their efficient and economic use? ☐
  - – and where these fuels come from? ☐

**Unit** ........................ **Date** ........................

## Learning

**Using investigations based on this unit, have the children demonstrated that they:**

**Level 1**

AT 5 • know that human activities produce a wide range of waste products? ☐

**Level 2**

AT 5 • know that some waste products decay naturally but often do so over a long period of time? ☐

• (can) keep a diary, in a variety of forms, of change over time? ☐

AT 16 • know that we live on a large 'spherical' self-contained planet, called Earth? ☐

**Level 3**

AT 5 • know that human activity may produce local changes in the Earth's surface? ☐

– air? ☐

– and water? ☐

• (can) give an account of a project to help improve the local environment? ☐

AT 6 • know that some materials occur naturally while many are made from raw materials? ☐

**Level 4**

AT 5 • know that some waste materials can be recycled? ☐

AT 13 • understand that energy is essential to every aspect of human life and activity? ☐

• know that there is a range of fuels which can be used to provide energy? ☐

AT 2 • understand the key factors in the process of decay (temperature, microbes, compactness, moisture) and how this is important in the re-use of biological material in everyday life? ☐

**Level 5**

AT 5 • (can) describe the sources (of pollution)? ☐

– the implications (of pollution)? ☐

– and the possible effects of pollution? ☐

• (can) classify waste products as biodegradable and non-biodegradable? ☐

• (can) argue for and against particular planning proposals in the locality, which may have an environmental impact? ☐

AT 13 • understand the need for fuel economy and efficiency? ☐

• understand the idea of global energy resources and appreciate that these resources are limited? ☐

See AT 1 evaluation checklist (page 11).

# UNIT 5
# OUR BODIES

## Opportunities for learning

Working from this unit, children will be developing their investigative skills and their knowledge and understanding of:

- the organisation of living things and of the processes which characterise their survival and reproduction
- variation, its genetic and environmental causes and the basic mechanisms of inheritance
- the nature of energy

For greater detail, refer to the evaluation checklist (teaching) at the end of this unit.

## Topics

| | |
|---|---|
| **MOVEMENT** | Messages<br>Change ( age–related )<br>Moods / behaviour |
| **FOOD** | Shopping<br>Diet<br>Materials |

## Cross-curricular links

| | |
|---|---|
| **ART / CRAFT** | Cultural variations |
| **ENGLISH** | Cultural differences in written language |
| **GEOGRAPHY** | Cultural differences relating to food<br>Tracing favourite foods to find out where they come from ( using the labelling ) |
| **HISTORY** | How people used to think that diseases were transmitted |
| **MATHEMATICS** | Measurement, volume, handling data, using and applying mathematics<br>12 M 3 : Personal data such as height and date of birth;<br>14 M 1 : Simple random events such as a new baby being either a boy or a girl;<br>12 M 5 : Draw conclusions from census data about the effect of an epidemic |
| **PERSONAL / SOCIAL EDUCATION** | Opportunities to link with broader school policy |
| **P E** | Moving together: for example, a three-legged race; picking up equipment together |
| **TECHNOLOGY** | Designing 'systems' for safe movement, for example, round the school |

## Classroom materials

The following *Nelson Science* materials support this unit:

**Picture Resource Book 2**

- p.1, 2, 4, 5 – family groups
- p.3 – the skeleton
- p.4, 5 – the social aspects of food
- p.6 – the dentist
- p.7 – the eye
- p.21 – fresh food, moulds

**Science Explorers**

- **Carrying Out Surveys 1, 2 and 3**
- **Experimenting 1, 2 and 3**
- **Problem Solving 1, 2 and 3**

M Sleap, J Perch, P Warburton: *Happy Heart 2* (Nelson)

Information on the heart, lungs, muscles and bones in relation to physical activity may be requested from the Health Education Authority, Hamilton House, Mabledon Place, London WC1H 9TX.

## Related units

### Units in the Teacher's Classroom Manual (Key Stage 2)

- The local environment and beyond - Unit 4
- Living things in the local environment - Unit 7
- How animals work - Unit 8
- Measuring the weather - Unit 9

### Units in the Teacher's Classroom Manual (Key Stage 1)

- Growing and moving - Unit 5
- Using the senses - Unit 6
- Feeding - Unit 7

## Resources and equipment

- a 3-litre plastic lemonade bottle and a sink or bowl of water
- a rubber tube and wipes to clean one end
- games equipment, for example, skipping ropes and balls
- bathroom scales
- 'everyday' things for experiments on the sense of smell, for example, coffee, an orange, soap, water
- 'everyday' things for experiments on the sense of hearing, for example, peas, paperclips, cotton wool, a rubber
- X-ray plates
- a clinical thermometer (spirit-filled or liquid crystal strips)
- a stop-watch
- coins for flipping
- reference books which include information about white blood corpuscles, antibodies and viruses

## Safety

Ensure that the children:

- never smell or taste things out of unfamiliar bottles
- tell you about any medical problems
- use only sterilised mouthpieces

## Starting points

### The school environment

- children feeling out of breath in the playground or during PE
- a contagious disease or parasite which the children and parents must be warned about, for example headlice
- school medicals
- milk teeth falling out
- assemblies
- 'healthy living' jingles or advertisements
- a survey into likes and dislikes, for example in poetry, music, television, books, art
- school dinner menus

### The social environment

- a family member or a friend in hospital, or a visit to the doctor or dentist
- a new baby in the family
- news items on famine
- visits to schools of deaf, dumb or blind people, or exchange visits with special schools
- advertisements in the media
- shopping
- adults on diets
- keep fit centres

### Further afield

- a visit to a sewage works
- a visit to a police station, looking at fingerprints if possible
- a visit to a supermarket, clinic or health centre

Also see 'Making connections'.

## Asking questions

### I wonder whether ...

- everyone sleeps?
- there is anything humans can do which other animals can't?
- we can improve our skills with practice?
- our height is a guide to our weight?
- some diets are healthier than others?
- our movements can give a message to others?
- everyone can roll their tongue into a tube?
- left-eyed people are left-handed?
- I get the same taste all over my tongue?
- my body is defending me from microbes in the air?
- all breakfast cereals give us the same amount of energy?

### What happens if ...

- I don't brush my teeth for twenty-four hours?
- I run twice round the playground?
- I try to walk a straight line blindfolded?
- one of our senses cannot be used?

## Gathering information

### Carrying out surveys

**Collecting information about:**

- the importance of sleep
- whether humans are as clever as they think they are by asking this question in reverse
- the variety of skills which can be improved with practice, and then considering which can be easily measured in terms of progress
- the heights and weights of the children in the class and presenting the results in the form of a scatter graph
- diet from as wide a variety of sources as possible
- how, for example, their moods are conveyed through their behaviour
- genetically determined traits which are easily investigated
- a simple test for eye dominance
- taste buds and trying to map the areas for sweet, sour and bitter tastes on the tongue
- why, if air is all around us and microbes are carried in it, we aren't ill all the time
- energy from the labels on cereal packets

### Experimenting

**Children:**

- can be introduced to disclosing tablets, constructing a fair test to determine the difference brushing teeth can make to plaque formation
- make qualitative measurements of the increase in their pulse rate as they become out of breath, and reflect on why this happens
- work co-operatively in groups to get the answer, and discuss the best way to record their results.
- as an extension of this activity, discuss whether it is easy to do without any of the senses, which are there to keep us safe

## Asking questions

### Can I find a way to ...

- measure my lung capacity?
- make a model which can move as a human does?
- work out how likely it is that a family will have the same number of boys and girls?

## Gathering information

### Solving practical problems

**Children:**

- demonstrate the displacement of water from a large, clear container inverted over a bowl, comparing their results with those of others in the class
- must first of all investigate how many joints they have in their limbs
- can imitate the probability (50:50) of a baby being a boy/girl by flipping a coin; the probability is not affected by the gender of siblings

Examples of ways in which these ideas have been developed in the classroom are provided on pages 76–81.

## Handling information

- Encourage systematic listing and recording of data:
  - frequency tables

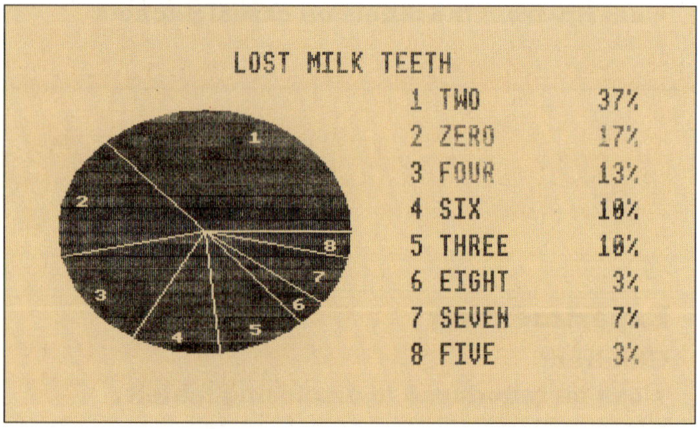


  - bar charts

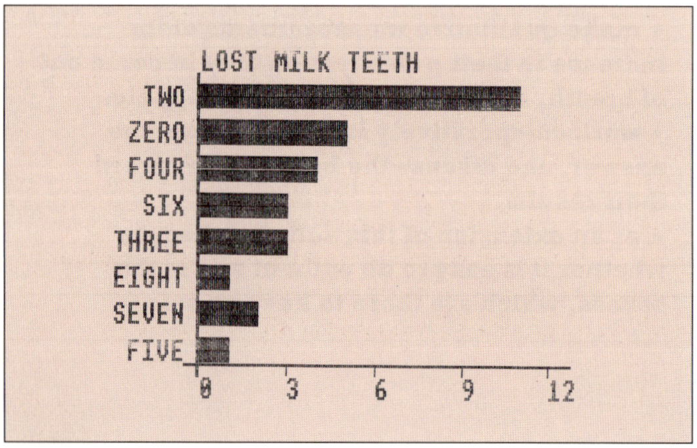


- Encourage searching for patterns in data.

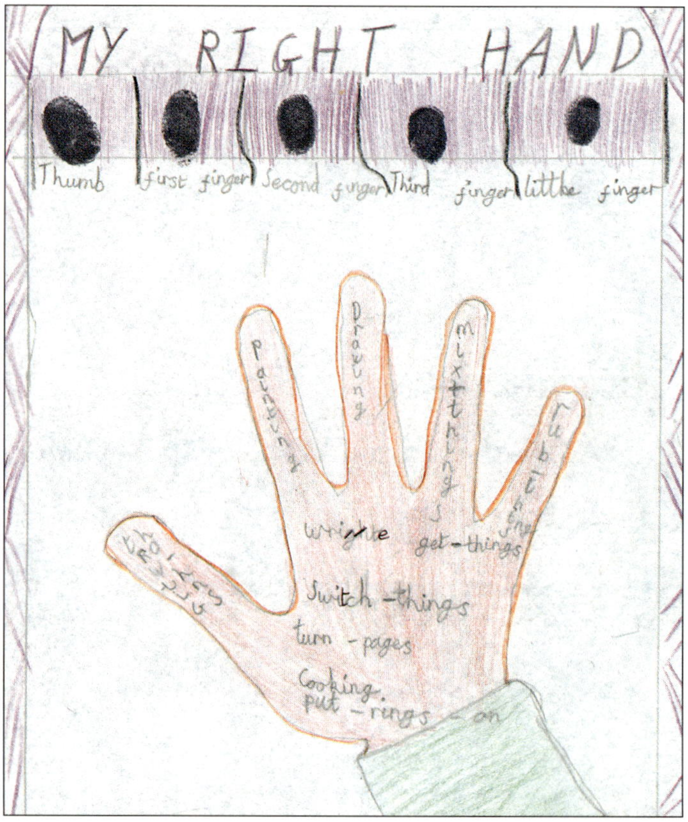


- Encourage written and/or oral reporting skills as appropriate.
- Encourage the use of a limited technical vocabulary in communicating findings and ideas.

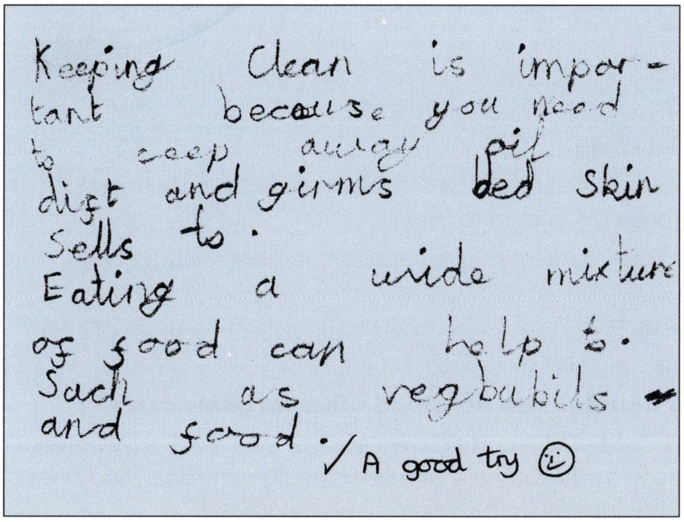


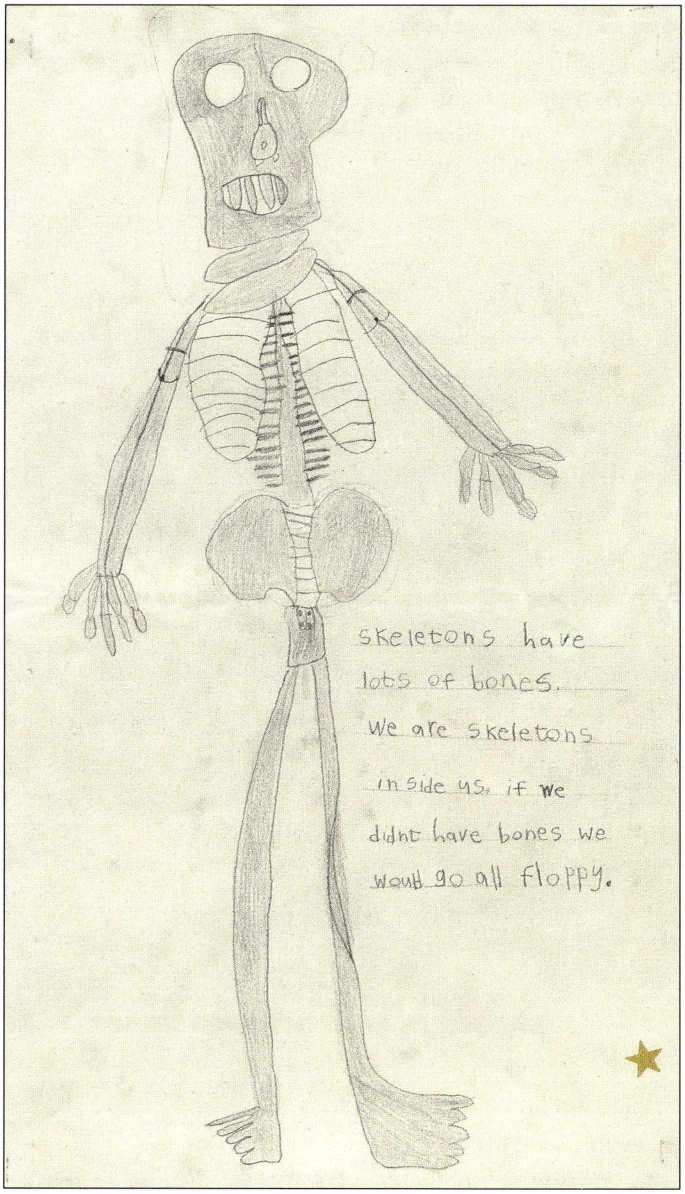


- Encourage the interpretation of data, and evaluation against the demands of the problem.

## Review points

The following are useful talking points:

### Our investigations

- new vocabulary we learned; for example: *preservation, genes, preference, culture, inherit, hereditary, disease, contagious, sterile, data, vaccination, antibiotic, virus, blood corpuscle, antibody, mucus, scab, acid, alkali, neutral, infectious, non-infectious*; can we add to our definitions?
- the questions we raised that we answered, and those we must leave unanswered
- the variables we controlled, and those we should have or would like to have controlled
- the new equipment we used, or skills we learned; were we successful? do we need more practice?
- any patterns we noticed in the data or tentative hypotheses we made

### Making connections

- sweating and the importance of salt and water in our body chemistry
- the importance of a clean water supply and the need to wash our hands
- the filtering of the blood in the kidneys, for example, may be explained by a comparison with the filters used in cleaning dirty water
- diet and the care of teeth
- movement and age; leisure activities become less vigorous but are nevertheless important
- movement and safety; crowds can be dangerous, and therefore barriers are used to divide them into smaller groups (rules for the school corridors?)
- movement to convey messages: semaphore, deaf and dumb sign language, mime artists; historical links, for example, the thumbs up sign in the Roman amphitheatre
- hereditary diseases, for example haemophilia; links with family as well as royal history
- the history of health care: the story of Eyam; the discovery of penicillin or the first vaccinations
- life support machines; the need for divers, astronauts, high altitude pilots and submarines to carry oxygen
- food as fuel for living and working
- reaction times and road safety; the Red Arrows

## Investigations

### I wonder whether ...

- **everyone sleeps?**

This investigation could cover:

– night jobs such as those of police officers, fishermen, lorry drivers and nurses, and the time these people go to bed

– different sorts of bed the children may have slept in: bunks, single beds, hammocks, lilos

– night creatures such as owls, hedgehogs and bats; collect pictures of living things asleep, or things they sleep on or in

- **there is anything humans can do which other animals can't?**

The difference usually cited is that humans can control their own environment. However, examples such as threading a needle, playing a musical instrument, walking on the moon and having ambitions may be discussed.

- **we can improve our skills with practice?**

Examples include releasing and re-catching a 15 cm ruler between thumb and forefinger with improvements measured in centimetres; skipping, swimming, ball bouncing, throwing or catching. What are the implications of any patterns in the results?

This could be linked to reaction times and road safety.

- **our height is a guide to our weight?**

Children make a hypothesis and then test it by reference to a scatter graph.

- **some diets are healthier than others?**

Children could send away for data, or gather information about diet from magazines, newspapers and supermarkets. Interpreting the information on food packaging could lead to investigations about food additives and whether they are always necessary, allergies and special diets, for example, for diabetic children. This work can link with the English curriculum.

Talk about different cultures, countries and religions, and cost considerations.

Link to Unit 8 'How animals work' and the diets of wild animals and/ or pets.

- **our movements can give a message to others?**

Link this to personal and social education and how we convey our feelings.

The messages conveyed by clapping, smiling, waving and shaking hands may be interpreted differently in different countries. Talk about mime artists, sign language and semaphore.

- **everyone can roll their tongue into a tube?**

Children can either do this or they can't; it is not a skill which can be improved through practice.

Children could work out which group is in the majority (the dominant trait) after testing as wide a sample as possible.

Other easily investigated, genetically determined traits include the attachment of ear lobes (they may be fixed or free), the ability to smell freesias, and eye colour.

- **left-eyed people are left-handed?**

One simple test for eye dominance is to line up a pencil with a straight edge, such as a door frame or a window, using both eyes. Then close one eye at a time. The pencil will jump to one side with one eye, showing that the closed eye was the one most used when lining up the pencil.

Is there a link with the hand the child uses for writing?

Extend the investigation to considerations of eye care.

- **I get the same taste all over my tongue?**

Children should design this experiment carefully to take full account of hygiene. They could use sugar, salt, vinegar and cocoa powder as standards before trying a variety of favourites.

This experiment lends itself to a consideration of the need for indicators. Encourage children to reflect that we may wish to know whether or not something is acid, but we certainly would not wish to taste it to gain this information.

The water left from boiling a red cabbage or beetroot provides an indicator for acidity. (Or use the liquid from a jar of pickled red cabbage.)

The base cut from a plastic lemonade bottle is ideal for this. Children could add vinegar dropwise to a section containing the indicator, and observe and record.

Reflect that the stomach needs to be a little acid to help digest food, but if it is too acid it gives us indigestion, so we take something to neutralise the acid. (A neutral solution is neither acid nor alkali.) Add an indigestion remedy dropwise to the indicator in another section and observe.

Washing soda will also provide the opposite of acid (alkali). Children could find out from secondary sources about the extreme danger to skin and clothes of strong acids or alkalis. Talk about their use in industry.

If litmus paper is available, children could be told that this is also a plant dye, from lichens.

The acid/ alkali indicator could help classify `Everyday kitchen powders'; for example, sodium bicarbonate fizzes in acid.

- **my body is defending me from microbes in the air?**

Children could reflect on the defence offered by their skin, and substances such as wax and mucus which we only tend to notice if the cells producing them become infected. Starting from their own experience of scabs, which form to protect our bodies when the skin is damaged, children could find out about platelets and white blood corpuscles from secondary sources. This could be extended to finding out about antibodies, vaccinations and antibiotics. Talk about viruses and other ways in which diseases may be transmitted.

- **all breakfast cereals give us the same amount of energy?**

This investigation could be expanded into a survey of a wide variety of food labels and the information which can be gained by interpreting them.

## What happens if ...

- **I don't brush my teeth for twenty-four hours?**

Children set up a control group. How do they ensure a fair test when using disclosing tablets?

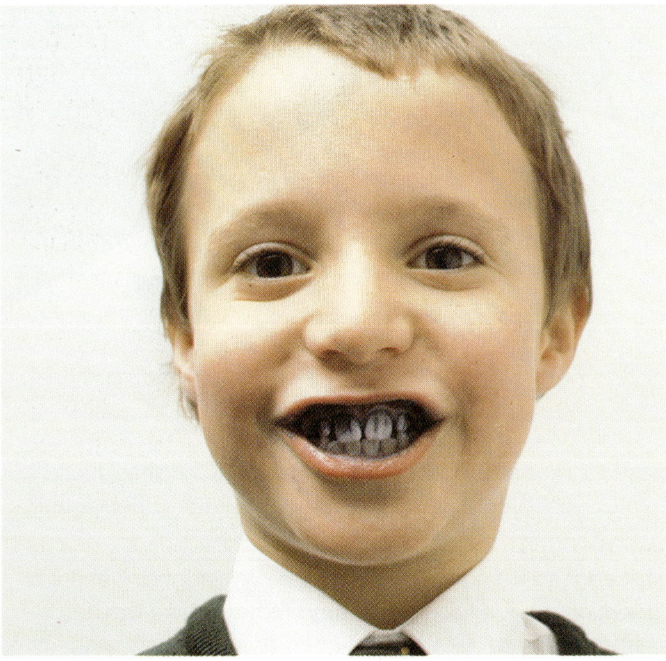

- **I run twice round the playground?**

Children may reflect that it is hard not to alter their breathing rate when someone is watching, timing and counting. Reading the pulse rate may therefore be a more accurate measure of the body trying to take in more oxygen through the lungs and pump it to the muscles.

The more work done, the more energy is used.

This investigation could link to the importance of oxygen and the 'burning' of food (fuel) to do work which makes us feel warmer. The waste from this `burning' of fuel is taken away in the blood. However, if we eat too much, carrying the excess weight is like carrying a heavy bag all day.

- **I try to walk a straight line blindfolded?**

If the straight line is chalked on the ground, the line actually travelled can be drawn by a partner. (Use a string if marking the ground is problematic.) What does it feel like to be unable to see?

- **one of our senses cannot be used?**

Try putting things into groups using the sense of touch only.

Try identifying objects in containers using only the sense of hearing or smell. (Try cheese, grass, vinegar, cotton wool, tea, a paperclip.) Record children's predictions. Pay due regard to safety considerations.

## Can I find a way to ...

- **measure my lung capacity?**

Mark a series of units on the side of a 3-litre lemonade bottle.

Fill to capacity with water, insert a long rubber tube, then invert over a (half-full) bowl of water. Record how much gas a child can expel with one breath.

How many turns should be allowed for each child?

What rules are needed to make it fair?

Reflect that not all the gas can be expelled from the lungs; some must be left behind. Remember to sterilise the rubber tube/mouthpiece after each use.

- **make a model which can move as a human does?**

Children could find out about the skeleton, which allows them to move through a system of joints, muscles and nerves controlled by the brain.

Reflect that this framework is also for the support and protection of their softer organs.

This investigation may be extended by constructing a paper skeleton or borrowing a plastic one.

- **work out how likely it is that a family will have the same number of boys and girls?**

A very simple explanation of the theory of genetics is that each individual has two genes which code for a particular trait, such as hair or eye colour (or the ability to roll the tongue). One gene is inherited from the father and one from the mother. The gene which dominates the pair will affect the outward appearance of the offspring. For example, the gene for dark eyes is 'dominant'; the gene for blue eyes is therefore 'recessive' and blue eyes will only appear if both of an individual's genes are recessive for that trait.

Females have two X genes. Males have an X and a Y gene.

The baby could therefore have two X genes and be female, or an XY pair and be male. This is analogous to flipping a coin. If individual children accurately record the result of ten flips of a coin, they are unlikely to get 50:50 results (compare with all girl or all boy families). The figures should get closer to 50:50 if the results of the whole class are pooled (compare with the male/female ratio in a whole population).

**Unit** ........................ **Date** ........................

## Teaching

**Have the children been provided with opportunities to:**

- work on questions or problems which they have accepted as their own? ☐
- develop their skills of exploration and investigation? ☐

See AT 1 evaluation checklist (page 11).

**Has the work pupils were engaged in allowed them to:**

PS 3
- investigate some aspects of:
  - feeding? ☐
  - support? ☐
  - movement? ☐
  - behaviour in relation to themselves and other animals? ☐
- be introduced to:
  - the functions of the major organ systems? ☐
  - the processes of breathing? ☐
  - the circulation of the blood? ☐
  - growth? ☐
  - reproduction? ☐
- explore ways in which good health can be promoted in relation to their own daily routine, using a range of secondary sources chosen by the teacher? ☐
- be introduced to the fact that whilst all medicines are drugs, not all drugs are medicines? ☐
- begin to be aware of the catastrophic effect on health of an abuse of drugs? ☐

PS 4
- investigate similarities and differences between themselves? ☐

PHOTOCOPY

**Unit ......................** **Date ......................**

## Learning

**Using investigations based on this unit, have the children demonstrated that they:**

**Level 1**

AT 2 • know that there is a wide variety of living things, which includes human beings? ☐

AT 3 • (can) name or label the external parts of the human body, for example, *arm, leg*? ☐

AT 4 • know that human beings vary from one individual to the next? ☐

AT 13 • understand that they need food to be active? ☐

• (can) describe, by talking or other appropriate means, how food is necessary for life? ☐

**Level 2**

AT 2 • know that plants and animals need certain conditions to sustain life? ☐

AT 3 • know that living things reproduce their own kind? ☐

• know that personal hygiene, food, exercise, rest and safety, and the proper safe use of medicines are important? ☐

• (can) give a simple account of the pattern of their own day? ☐

AT 4 • (can) measure simple differences between each other? ☐

AT 5 • (can) keep a diary, in a variety of forms, of change over time? ☐

**Level 3**

AT 2 • (can) recognise similarities and differences among living things? ☐

• (can) sort living things into broad groups according to observable features? ☐

AT 3 • know that the basic life processes:

– feeding ☐

– breathing ☐

– movement ☐

– and behaviour, are common to human beings and the other living things they have studied? ☐

• (can) describe the main stages in the human life cycle? ☐

AT 13 • know that temperature is a measure of how hot (or cold) things are? ☐

**Level 4**

AT 3 • (can) name the major organs and organ systems in mammals? ☐

• know about the factors which contribute to good health and body maintenance:

– including the defence systems of the body? ☐

– balanced diet? ☐

– oral hygiene? ☐

– and avoidance of harmful substances such as tobacco, alcohol and other drugs? ☐

AT 4 • (can) measure variations in living organisms? ☐

AT 13 • understand that energy is essential to every aspect of human life and activity? ☐

• (can) measure temperature using a thermometer? ☐

**Level 5**

AT 3 • know that living things are made up from different kinds of cells which carry out different jobs? ☐

• understand malnutrition? ☐

– and the relationships between diet, exercise, health, fitness and circulatory disorders? ☐

• know that in digestion food is made soluble so that it can enter the blood? ☐

• understand the way in which microbes ... ☐

... and lifestyle affect health? ☐

• (can) describe the functions of the major organ systems? ☐

AT 4 • know that information in the form of genes is passed on from one generation to the next? ☐

AT 6 • (can) classify aqueous solutions as acidic, alkaline or neutral, by using indicators? ☐

See AT 1 evaluation checklist (page 11).

# UNIT 6
# HOW FLOWERING PLANTS WORK

## Opportunities for learning

Working from this unit, children will be developing their knowledge and understanding of:

- the organisation of living things
- the processes which characterise their survival and reproduction
- ways in which human activities affect the Earth
- the nature of energy

For greater detail, refer to the evaluation checklist (teaching) at the end of this unit.

## Topics

| | |
|---|---|
| **FESTIVALS** | Flower festivals in this country and elsewhere |
| **THE SEASONS** | Gardens |
| **ENERGY / FUELS** | Warmth and growth rates |
| **REPRODUCTION IN PLANTS** | |

## Cross-curricular links

| | |
|---|---|
| **ART** | 'Design' ideas in flowers; colour |
| **GEOGRAPHY** | Plants for food in different countries and cultures |
| **MATHEMATICS** | Percentage germination rates<br>'Costings' if plants are to be sold |
| **TECHNOLOGY** | Plant structures; strength in stem shapes<br>Systems to prevent plants drying out over half-term |

## Classroom materials

The following *Nelson Science* materials support this unit:

**Picture Resource Book 1**

- p.8, 9, 10 and cover – the structure of different trees and seasonal changes
- p.1 – a composite flower, a near relative of the dandelion, clearly showing that each flower head is made up of numerous little flowers; each floret produces a seed at the base of the 'parachute'
- p.2 – the bee; where do insects fit into the above cycles?

- p.9 – another composite flower, the chamomile; each 'petal' is a modified floret
- p.6, 7, 11 – the life cycle of insect-pollinated flowering plants

**Picture Resource Book 2**

- p.16 – an insect feeding on the nectar of buddleia

**Science Explorers**

- **Carrying Out Surveys 1, 2 and 3**
- **Experimenting 1, 2 and 3**
- **Problem Solving 1, 2 and 3**

## Related units

### Units in the Teacher's Classroom Manual (Key Stage 2)

- The local environment and beyond – Unit 4
- Our bodies – Unit 5
- Living things in the local environment – Unit 7
- Weathering, minerals, rocks and soil – Unit 12

### Units in the Teacher's Classroom Manual (Key Stage 1)

- How to take care of plants – Unit 8
- How plant life varies – Unit 9
- Seasonal and daily changes in plants – Unit 10

## Resources and equipment

- plants for cuttings, for example: begonia, ivy, 'Busy Lizzie', geranium (pelargonium)
- a 'wild' seed collection, especially including: sycamore, poppy, dandelion, rose-bay willow herb
- commercially produced seed packets (even outdated ones), especially those for beans and peas, mung beans
- bird seed
- a variety of pots and tubs, or plastic food containers with drainage holes
- a variety of tools to help grow plants, for example, hand forks, dibbers, flatteners
- potting compost
- magnifying glasses
- fresh, easily obtainable, light coloured stems, for example, celery
- aluminium foil

### Safety

Ensure that the children:

- are warned about poisonous plants or parts of plants
- know that it is illegal intentionally to uproot any plant grown in the wild unless it is on your own land or you have obtained permission
- know that there are also certain specially protected plants; it is illegal to pick, uproot, destroy or collect their flowers or seeds

## Starting points

### The school environment

- a patch of playing field where the grass is allowed to seed, or a seed collection
- pot plants in the classroom (investigations from this unit lend themselves to mini-enterprise schemes to raise funds)
- slides, photos or videos, especially where time-lapse photography is involved

### The social environment

- supermarkets or fruit and vegetable shops; notice the exotic fruits and link to food preferences in different cultures
- gardens, garden centres, allotments and other examples of cultivated ground
- wildlife parks

### Further afield

- any habitat which is different from the child's everyday experience, particularly where there is a change of climate
- the experiences of a child who has travelled abroad
- a natural history museum

Also see 'Making connections'.

## Asking questions

**I wonder whether ...**

- **all flowers are pollinated by insects?**
- **all roots are the same shape?**
- **all seeds look the same?**
- **there is a reason why seeds vary so much?**
- **the age of the seeds makes any difference to how they grow?**
- **plants which live on Earth have always looked like this?**

## Gathering information

**Carrying out surveys**

**Children:**

- **observe flowers at first hand and from secondary sources:**
  - **finding out if they are all brightly coloured, are scented, have nectar**
  - **finding out what visits them and why**
- **wash the roots of weeds from the school garden or flower tubs, observing, recording and comparing to a food root, for example, a carrot**
- **investigate a bird seed mixture, making and labelling a collection of as many kinds of seed as possible**
- **make predictions, using observations about the appearance of seeds (especially from a 'wild' seed collection) on the way in which seeds are dispersed**
- **plant commercially packaged seeds of different ages under the same (ideal) conditions and compare their germination rates**
- **gather information about fossils, the formation of coalfields and plant species which are becoming extinct in the tropical rainforests**

## Asking questions

### What happens if ...

- I carefully open a bean seed?
- I gently place a pencil or finger on the 'platform' of an antirrhinum (snapdragon) flower?
- I vary the conditions for germinating seeds?

## Gathering information

### Experimenting

Children:

- open a broad bean seed which has been soaked overnight, using a magnifying glass to observe the embryo plant
- carefully simulate an insect landing on flowers, especially those with platforms, observing closely
- grow seeds from the same packet, varying conditions of heat, water, compost, light and dark, and compare results; try using liquid fertiliser, ranging from none to a high concentration

### Can I find a way to ...

- grow a new plant without having a seed?
- show that water is given out by the leaves of a plant?
- show that a stem has particular cells which take up water?
- show that a plant needs sunlight?
- make the seedlings on a windowsill grow up straight?

### Solving practical problems

Children:

- take cuttings from, for example, a geranium, a 'Busy Lizzie', or ivy; find other suitable species using secondary sources
- gently seal some leaves from a strongly growing plant in a clear plastic bag, taking care not to damage the plant; use sellotape to seal the bag round the base of the leaves
- place some long, pale coloured stems (for example, celery) in water to which a contrasting colour has been added
A stem should be placed horizontally (fair testing) as well as upright. Leave and observe.
- cover single leaves of a bushy, actively growing plant with paper which does not allow the light through; leave for a week, uncover and observe
– or take some identical plants from germination experiments, and place some in strong sunlight, some in shade and some in a cupboard
- design and construct a three-sided surround to help seedlings to grow straight, using children's experience of reflective surfaces

Examples of ways in which these ideas have been developed in the classroom are provided on pages 89–93.

## Handling information

- Encourage systematic listing and recording of data:
  - frequency tables

  - bar charts
- Encourage searching for patterns in data.

- Encourage written and/or oral reporting skills as appropriate.
- Encourage the use of a limited technical vocabulary in communicating findings and ideas.
- Encourage the interpretation of data, and evaluation against the demands of the problem.

## Review points

The following are useful talking points:

### Our investigations

- new vocabulary we learned; for example: *ovary, stamens, stigma, pollen, egg, embryo, fertilisation, surface, dispersal, nourish, fertiliser, temperature, moisture, annual, perennial, variation, photosynthesis;* can we add to our definitions?
- the questions we raised that we answered, and those we must leave unanswered
- the variables we controlled, and those we should have or would like to have controlled
- the new equipment we used, or skills we learned; were we successful? do we need more practice?
- any patterns we noticed in the data or tentative hypotheses we made

### Making connections

- hay fever – an allergic reaction to large quantities of pollen from wind-pollinated flowers; at certain times of the year, the pollen count is broadcast to warn sufferers
- flowers, such as some orchids, attract insects not by offering food substances, but by imitating the female insect and encouraging the male to mate; children could find out about these and other specialised pollination mechanisms
- harmful plants, such as tobacco
- edible plants
- movement in plants, including
  - the response of crocuses and tulips to a rise or fall in temperature
  - night-scented stock which is closed by day, but open and strongly fragrant at night because it is pollinated by night-flying moths

## Investigations

### I wonder whether ...

- **all flowers are pollinated by insects?**

Children survey flowers they can see in the locality, and then reflect on what they have in common: bright colours, scent, nectaries, stamens, ovaries, for example.

Children could sit and observe visitors to the flowers.

Depending on the season, children could observe hazel catkins or a variety of grasses, reflecting on the fact that these too are flowers.

Look for differences between these and insect-pollinated plants, for example, the amount and appearance of the pollen and the prominence of the flowers.

(In the case of hazel, the female parts are on a separate, quite different flower.)

The male parts have to be dangly and feathery and the pollen light so that it can be carried in the wind.

Reflect that the purpose of a flower is to ensure the fertilisation of the egg by the pollen.

- **all roots are the same shape?**

Children carefully dig up a weed, wash it, lay it out on newspaper and measure the area covered, the length of the longest rootlet, and, where appropriate, the diameter of the thickest.

Compare the roots of 'weeds', for example, a dandelion and a daisy.

Reflect on what roots are for: support and anchorage, taking up water and nutrients and sometimes for food storage.

- **all seeds look the same?**

Using a bird seed mixture, children observe, sort, count and measure. Reflect on what seeds are for: protecting and nourishing the embryo plant.

- **there is a reason why seeds vary so much?**

Children use magnifying glasses to investigate a collection of 'wild' plant seeds and seed containers. They may be eaten, explode, shake out from 'pepper pots', hook on to animals, or float off in water.

Wind-dispersed seeds may blow away like dust, have parachutes or be shaped like spinners.

- **the age of the seeds makes any difference to how they grow?**

Plant bird seed (or other cheaply available seeds) in compost to record which seeds germinate and how many. If appropriate, the number of seeds may be carefully counted, and the percentage of seeds which germinate calculated.

- **plants which live on Earth have always looked like this?**

Children could gather information on coal as an ancient form of plant life, and reflect on the impossibility of there being more fuel from this source.Talk about the extinction of species.

### What happens if ...

- **I carefully open a bean seed?**

The embryo plant can be seen between the two halves of the food store which will nourish it until it can produce its own food. Find other seeds in which the embryo plant can be clearly seen, for example, the pea or the peanut.

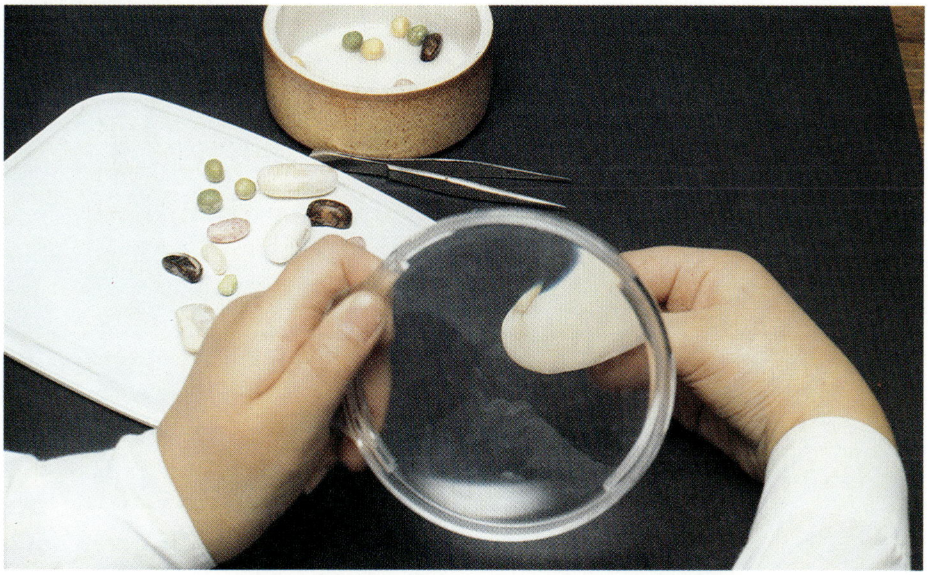

- **I gently place a pencil or finger on the platform of an antirrhinum?**

The antirrhinum is a common flower which has a distinct 'landing stage' to encourage the insect to place its body in just the right place for pollination. Another example is the foxglove.

Observe what happens when the insect flies on to the next flower.

Reflect on why it is important for the pollen from one flower to reach another.

- **I vary the conditions for germinating seeds?**

Gently remove the seedling from the soil at least once per week, and measure the root length and spread. Record in the form of a graph.

### Can I find a way to ...

- **grow a new plant without having a seed?**

Gather information about taking and growing stem, root and leaf cuttings.

- **show that water is given out by the leaves of a plant?**

The inside of the plastic bag will become covered in moisture; the time taken will depend on the conditions.

Discuss the limitations of the experiment.

- **show that a stem has particular cells which take up water?**

The stem lengths which have been standing vertically should have distinct lines of colour through them showing the vascular bundles, especially if some leaves were left in place. Talk about why the stems are not uniformly coloured, cutting cross sections if necessary. The stems which were laid horizontally in the liquid will look very different, especially if their cut ends were out of the liquid.

- **show that a plant needs sunlight?**

Remove the opaque paper and observe the leaf. This should look sickly and yellow, but may recover in a few days.

Predict what would happen to a whole plant under these conditions and try it, disposable plant supply permitting. This investigation could be extended to a consideration of the photosynthesising plant as something upon which all other living things depend. It is a storehouse of fuel for energy and produces oxygen.

- **make the seedlings on a windowsill grow up straight?**

Cut away one side of an orange box and line the other three on the inside with aluminium foil. Place the seed tray in the box. These seedlings will grow straighter than those in a control.

Reflect on the importance of light to plants, and gather information about photosynthesis, the process by which green plants, in the presence of sunlight and chlorophyll, convert carbon dioxide and water into food with oxygen as a waste product.

**Unit ......................** **Date ......................**

# Teaching

**Have the children been provided with opportunities to:**

- work on questions or problems which they have accepted as their own? ☐
- develop their skills of exploration and investigation? ☐

See AT 1 evaluation checklist (page 11).

**Has the work pupils were engaged in allowed them to:**

PS 2
- explore and investigate at least two different localities and the ways in which plants and animals are suited to their location? ☐
- explore some ways in which plant behaviour and life cycles are influenced by:
  - – environmental conditions? ☐
  - – seasonal changes? ☐
  - – daily changes? ☐
- explore the range of past life forms preserved as fossils, using:
  - – secondary sources? ☐
  - – specimens (if possible)? ☐
- develop skills in identifying locally occurring species of plants, marking these against keys, using observable structural features of organisms:
  - – at first hand? ☐
  - – through sources provided by the teacher? ☐
  - – with increasing independence in the use of sources? ☐
  - – with developing awareness and understanding of the necessity for sensitive:
    - – collection? ☐
    - – and care of living things used as the subject of any study of the environment? ☐

PS 3
- investigate the effects of physical factors on the rate of plant growth, for example:
  - – light intensity? ☐
  - – temperature? ☐
  - – the amount of fertiliser? ☐

PS 4
- measure the similarities and differences between accessible plants and fossil counterparts? ☐

Did the study cover extinct life forms and include basic ideas about genetic and environmental causes? ☐

Was attention given to the welfare and protection of living material? ☐

**Unit ........................** **Date ........................**

# Learning

**Using investigations based on this unit, have the children demonstrated that they:**

**Level 1**

AT 2 • know that there is a wide variety of living things, which includes human beings? ☐

AT 3 • are able to name or label the external parts of plants? ☐

**Level 2**

AT 2 • know that plants and animals need certain conditions to sustain life? ☐

• understand how living things are looked after and be able to treat them with care and consideration? ☐

AT3 • know that living things reproduce their own kind? ☐

AT 5 • (can) keep a diary, in a variety of forms, of change over time? ☐

**Level 3**

AT 2 • (can) recognise similarities and differences among living things? ☐

• (can) sort living things into broad groups according to observable features? ☐

• know that living things respond to seasonal and daily change? ☐

AT 3 • know that the basic life processes: feeding, breathing, movement and behaviour, are common to the living things they have studied? ☐

AT 4 • know that some life forms became extinct long ago and others more recently? ☐

**Level 4**

AT 2 • (can) recognise similarities and differences both within and between groups of plants? ☐

• understand that plants and animals can be preserved as fossils in different ways? ☐

AT 3 • (can) name the major organs and organ systems in flowering plants? ☐

• (can) describe the main stages of flowering plant reproduction? ☐

AT 4 • (can) measure variations in living organisms? ☐

**Level 5**

AT 2 • understand that the differences in physical factors between localities, including differences in seasonal and daily changes, are reflected in the different species of plants found there? ☐

• (can) assign organisms to their major groups using keys and observable features? ☐

• (can) support their view about environmental issues concerned with the use of fertilisers in agriculture and horticulture, based on their practical experience? ☐

• understand predator-prey relationships? ☐

AT 3 • know that living things are made up from different kinds of cells which carry out different jobs? ☐

• (can) describe the functions of the major organ systems? ☐

AT 4 • know that information in the form of genes is passed on from one generation to the next? ☐

See AT 1 evaluation checklist (page 11.)

# UNIT 7
# LIVING THINGS IN THE LOCAL ENVIRONMENT

## Opportunities for learning

Working from this unit, children will be developing their investigative skills and their knowledge and understanding of:

- variation and its genetic and environmental causes
- the relationships, energy flows, cycles of matter and human influences within ecosystems

For greater detail, refer to the evaluation checklist (teaching) at the end of this unit.

## Topics

| | |
|---|---|
| **HOMES / BUILDINGS** | Our school<br>Urban wildlife |
| **THE SEASONS / WEATHER** | Hibernation<br>Migration<br>Life cycles |
| **HABITATS** | Variety in and preservation of |
| **MINI-PLANTS** | Mosses, lichens, liverworts |
| **FOOD PRESERVATION** | Airborne organisms and health |

## Cross-curricular links

| | |
|---|---|
| **GEOGRAPHY** | Local effects of rainfall<br>Site conditions influencing temperature<br>Local windspeed and direction related to plant growth |
| **HISTORY** | Tracing back annual rings on a tree trunk |
| **MATHEMATICS** | Handling data<br>Constructing a frequency table for bird visits |
| **TECHNOLOGY** | Making bottle garden tools<br>Ways of collecting creatures without harming them |

## Classroom materials

The following *Nelson Science* materials support this unit:

**Picture Resource Book 1**

- p.1, 2, 7, 8, 13 – the dandelion, the bee, the tomato, the oak and a pollarded tree may all stimulate discussion

**Picture Resource Book 2**

- p.8, 12, 13, 15 – the fly, the cat, the frog, the squirrel
- p.9 – tropical fish
- p.14 – hedgehogs are insectivores, although they may eat some vegetable matter. What should we feed them and when?
- p.16 – this is an American Monarch butterfly. Children could find out about their migration. Do local species migrate at a particular time of year?
- p.21 – moulds, flowerless plants

**Picture Resource Book 3**

- p.17 – a sheep

**Science Explorers**

- **Carrying Out Surveys 1, 2 and 3**
- **Experimenting 1, 2 and 3**
- **Problem Solving 1, 2 and 3**

## Related units

### Units in the Teacher's Classroom Manual (Key Stage 2)

- Colour, mirrors, lenses and prisms – Unit 1
- Noise and music – Unit 2
- How animals work – Unit 8
- Measuring the weather – Unit 9
- Weathering, minerals, rocks and soil – Unit 12

### Units in the Teacher's Classroom Manual (Key Stage 1)

- How plant life varies – Unit 9
- Seasonal and daily changes in plants – Unit 10
- How animal life varies – Unit 12
- Seasonal and daily changes in animals – Unit 13

## Resources and equipment

- small tools such as trowels, lollipop sticks, old teaspoons
- protection for hands such as plastic or rubber gloves
- containers for transporting and planting and for temporary homes, for example: ice cream cartons, yoghurt pots, toffee tins with acetate sleeves
- assorted trays and white card for use while identifying specimens
- clean (or sterile) growing medium such as peat or potting compost
- large, clear glass bottles for bottle gardens, for example, demijohns
- a fine-spray watering can or a well cleaned spray-gun
- for a plant press: newspaper, paired flat pieces of hardboard, kilogram weights
- plastic or nylon netting with different kinds of mesh, for example: net curtaining, nylon tights, supermarket vegetable and fruit nets
- white sheeting
- good quality identification keys, for example the *Oxford Junior Clue* books

## Safety

Ensure that the children:
- are up to date with tetanus injections before experimenting with soil
- wear plastic gloves when touching plants on paths and roadways, or dealing with leaf litter where there is any danger of animals urinating or defecating, or of harmful moulds
- keep any moulds in the classroom sealed and dispose of them carefully

Read pages 11 and 13 of 'Be safe', published by the ASE.

## Starting points

### The school environment
- a ready made bottle garden
- moulds on and in food
- insects, spiders or other 'mini-beasts' in the classroom
- ground for making a 'wild area' or an allotment, or large tubs and window boxes

### The social environment
- gardens and other cultivated ground such as allotments or parks
- wasteland and woods
- garden centres

### Further afield
- farms, seashores, hedgerows, walls and soils
- botanical gardens

Also see 'Making connections'.

## Asking questions

### I wonder whether ...

• the direction in which a wall is facing affects the number of plants we find growing next to it?
• the height of a wall above ground level affects the number and variety of the plants?
• cracks between the paving stones support more types of plant than the surface of the stones?
• the paths we make when we walk affect the number or variety of the plants found there?

• we can keep a diary of our tree for a whole year?

• there are microbes in the soil?

• all spiders' webs are the same?

• slugs and snails like the same food?

### What happens if ...

• leaves are left on the ground for a long time?

• examples of the same species of plant are given different amounts of fertiliser?

• a caterpillar is put on a surface which is a different colour from its food?

## Gathering information

### Carrying out surveys

**Collecting information about:**

• the aspect of the wall, for example, the daily variations in sunlight, surface temperature and shading, and the proximity of free-standing plants
• the level on the wall at which plants occur; are there more at ground level than eye level?
• the length, depth and frequency of cracks and whether they are colonised or uncolonised

• a path which has been made over time by people walking across grass; the effect of this continual trampling on plant growth can be studied
• a tree carefully chosen by the children, ideally in the school grounds; discuss what, how and when to record
• decomposition and what happens to dead plant and animal matter left on the soil
• the habitat, food preferences and web types of the nearly 600 species of spider in Britain; ideal conditions for investigating spiders' webs occur on a misty or foggy day
• food preferences in slugs and snails of different shapes and sizes (They are not all vegetarians!)

### Experimenting

**Children:**

• collect fallen leaves of the same type and age and predict what will happen to them under different conditions
• choose easily available plants of the same species, size and age and treat them in the same way except that the dilution of liquid fertiliser is varied
• discuss the best time of year for collecting caterpillars; for example, oak trees are covered in larvae just as the bluetit fledglings need feeding

## Asking questions

### Can I find a way to ...

- start things growing on a bare wall?
- make a moss garden?
- find plants which will be suitable for a bottle garden?
- preserve the plants we have collected?
- make a good estimate of the different types of plant there are on our playing field?
- sample a pond without harming the animals?
- collect small land animals without harming them?
- find the conditions that woodlice prefer?

## Gathering information

### Solving practical problems

**Children:**

- investigate the problems faced by a plant growing on a wall, for example: texture and chemical make-up of the material, water supply
- plan how much of each specimen to use, depending on the size of the container (an ice cream box could be suitable)
- choose plants of a suitable size, and work out how to plant the bottle garden
- make a plant press
- use a simple quadrat, made by joining four pieces of wood to form a square frame
- construct a net which catches pond creatures for long enough to view them or transfer them to a viewing bowl without removing them from water
- design mini-beast transporters and catchers
- construct a choice chamber after observations in the field

Examples of ways in which these ideas have been developed in the classroom are provided on pages 102–107.

## Handling information

- Encourage systematic listing and recording of data:
  - frequency tables
  - bar charts
- Encourage searching for patterns in data.
- Encourage written and/or oral reporting skills as appropriate.

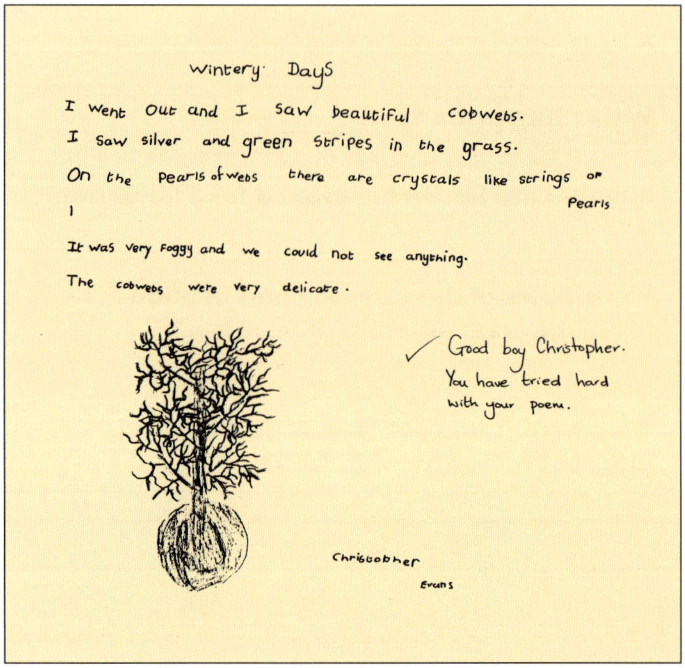
Wintery Days
I went out and I saw beautiful cobwebs.
I saw silver and green stripes in the grass.
On the pearls of webs there are crystals like strings of Pearls
It was very foggy and we could not see anything.
The cobwebs were very delicate.
✓ Good boy Christopher. You have tried hard with your poem.
Christobher Evans

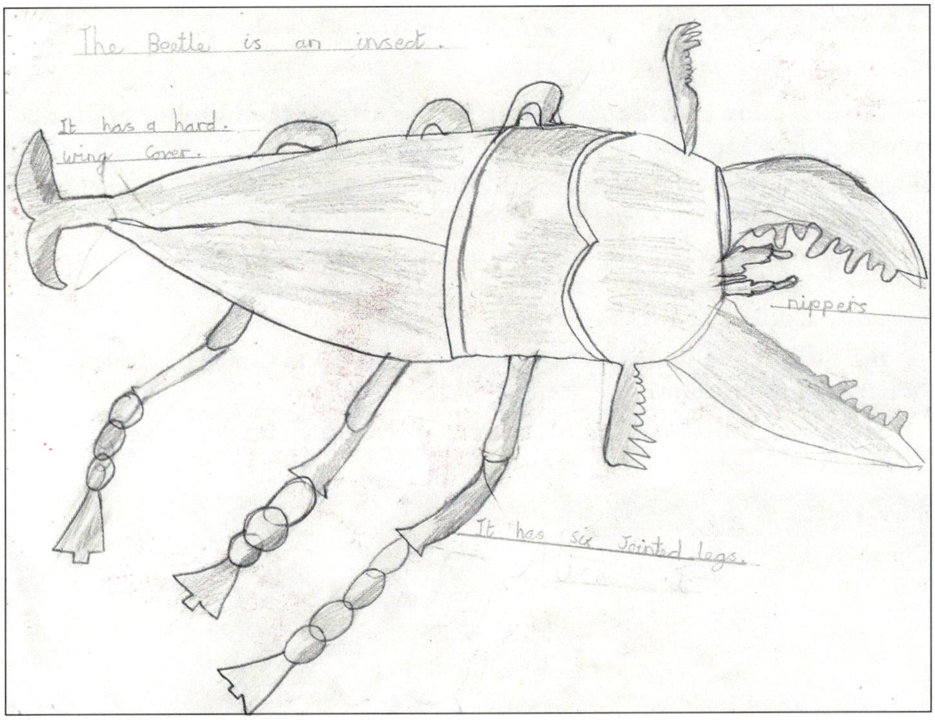


- Encourage the use of a limited technical vocabulary in communicating findings and ideas.
- Encourage the interpretation of data, and evaluation against the demands of the problem.

"Our plants died because Tracy put in too much water."

## Review points

The following are useful talking points:

### Our investigations

- new vocabulary we have learned; for example: *habitat, moisture, surface, microbes, decay, temperature, biological material, sterile, rotting, preserve, slime, shell, spiral, tentacle, enemy*; can we add to our definitions?
- the questions we raised that we answered, and those we must leave unanswered
- the variables we controlled, and those we should have or would like to have controlled
- the new equipment we used, or skills we learned; were we successful? do we need more practice?
- any patterns we noticed in the data or tentative hypotheses we made

### Making connections

- damage to walls by plants; physical damage by root systems and dampness caused by plant cover lead to the likelihood of further damage by frost
- deliberate 'ageing' of roofs and walls is sometimes desirable; why might we want to do this, and how can it be done?
- plants which are chosen to cover areas which sustain wear and tear or where the ground cover needs to be kept short, for example on playing fields
- the need for preserving food stuffs; methods include jam making, bottling, canning, salting, smoking and freezing
- useful microbes in cheese, yoghurt, milk and bread making
- writing for information from local or national wildlife organisations, especially about the winter feeding of birds
- looking for evidence of pollution in the local environment and reflecting on what action to take
- the danger to wildlife of litter, especially where bottles and cans can act as traps
- edible plants

## Investigations

### I wonder whether ...

- **the direction in which a wall is facing affects the number of plants we find growing next to it?**

Children can apply their skills of observation and recording of the weather to a specific part of their environment. For comparisons of surface and air temperature, aquarium thermometers (liquid crystal strips) can be used. Where a light meter is not available, squares of newspaper or coloured crepe can be affixed to the wall so that fading can be recorded.

- **the height of a wall above ground level affects the number and variety of the plants?**

By measuring, observing and counting plant types, a map of sample areas may be constructed.

- **cracks between the paving stones support more types of plant than the surface of the stones?**

Children quantify by measuring and recording the number of cracks in a given area.

They could then match to a count of the number and types of plants, for example lichens, mosses, ferns and flowering plants.

Children can draw inferences about why there are more plants in the cracks and use simple keys to identify types. This could lead to predictions of plant types to be found in a similar environment.

- **the paths we make when we walk affect the number or variety of the plants found there?**

Children could use simple quadrats to help record observations which include the height and spread of plants on and off the path as well as the presence and absence of different types. Recording could be done by drawing on squared paper. Examples of plants from the same species which have been continually trampled could be carefully lifted and taken back to the classroom for extensive measurement of their roots, stems and leaves. These results could be compared to the growth of examples of the same species carefully lifted from an untrampled area.

Children could record changes in the type and appearance of plants at agreed, marked intervals along a path.

- **we can keep a diary of our tree for a whole year?**

Draw a map of its position, girth, spread of branches and estimated age. Record its appearance in drawings, photographs, bark rubbings and plaster casts. Note its exposure to wind, sun and rain, and record the dates when:

– buds, leaves, flowers and seeds appear

– invertebrates and their eggs, larvae and pupae appear

– mammals and birds appear; record their behaviour over time, for example, are they visiting, feeding or living there?

Record and measure growth.

- **there are microbes in the soil?**

Items of fresh food could be placed on two disposable plates. One could be smeared with soil from the school grounds, and both be sealed into clear plastic containers and observed for about two weeks.

Children observe that there is an enormous concentration of microbes in soil and reflect on the importance of this observation. For example, without microbes, how would the nutrients be 'unlocked' from dead plants and animals?

- **all spiders' webs are the same?**

If appropriate, investigate 'nooks and crannies' in walls and behind cupboards. Damage prevention is all-important.

A cleaned scent atomiser may provide a spray of water fine enough to simulate mist and show up the structure of webs.

- **slugs and snails like the same food?**

Children could observe slugs and snails closely and make a table of similarities and differences. They could determine ideal conditions with two identical containers as temporary homes in which to keep the creatures for a few days. Design a fair test for their food preferences.

## What happens if ...

- **leaves are left on the ground for a long time?**

Ensure a fair test by carefully counting or weighing the leaves under experiment, or by cutting squares of identical size from the leaves. Depending on their predictions, children could vary the situation or the containers.

Identical leaf samples may be placed in nets made from the same non-biodegradable mesh, and left, for example, hanging from a tree, shallowly buried and buried deep in soil.

Samples can be buried to the same depth in nets made from different mesh, for example: tights, onion net, orange net and transparent film to exclude external agents.

Label all samples using insoluble ink. Observe and record at one or two-week intervals.

- **examples of the same species of plant are given different amounts of fertiliser?**

The easiest plant to choose is probably one of the species of duckweed obtained from a local pond or canal. The plants can be placed in different concentrations of liquid fertiliser in cut-off lemonade bottles. New plants can be counted and their numbers recorded as they multiply (after decisions have been made about what size 'counts' as a plant). What is the effect of far too much fertiliser?

- **a caterpillar is put on a surface which is a different colour from its food?**

A surprising number of different camouflage techniques may be observed in caterpillars collected from the grounds of most schools. Some caterpillars have warning coloration, and may stand out on their favourite food. For example, the stripy larvae of the cinnabar moth taste nasty to birds (their main predator). Other species have large eye spots.

If the life cycle of the insects is to be studied, design a suitable environment for them.

### Can I find a way to ...

- **start things growing on a bare wall?**

Design an experiment to determine how many seeds are carried to the wall through the air. For example, attach Vaseline-covered card to different parts of the wall and observe the 'catch' over a period of days. Reflect on the conditions which plants need to grow and consider how these may be simulated.

- **make a moss garden?**

Children should first consider collecting places and observe the variety of form and colour. Use a suitably sized container which will provide favourable conditions for growth.

- **find plants which will be suitable for a bottle garden?**

Having chosen a transparent bottle, children could design and make tools for planting, arranging and pruning. Small plants (in the light of experience with walls, cracks etc) can be chosen, or research into conventional bought varieties undertaken. Use paper funnels to get seeds in exactly the right spot.

- **preserve the plants we have collected?**

Children may use their understanding of the conditions for plant and mould growth to determine the necessity to dry the specimens. Lay the plants between sheets of newspaper, and place them between pieces of hardboard. Remind the children they are drying specimens, not crushing them!

**• make a good estimate of the different types of plant there are on our playing field?**

Using quadrats, children sample twenty times at random, then multiply proportionately.

**• sample a pond without harming the animals?**

Discuss with the children ways in which creatures living in the water surface, in the middle of the pond and on the bottom can be caught. Talk about sieves and nets with holes of different sizes, and ways in which the creatures can be caught without harming them.

**• collect small land animals without harming them?**

Three basic ideas can be developed:

– cut off the top of a clear plastic lemonade bottle below the point where it begins to narrow and invert it over its base. Fix it in place with four small strips of tape. Creatures smaller than the opening may be dropped into the container and observed at leisure, then released outside by removing the tape.

– sew nylon curtain netting over a wire coat-hanger, and attach the hanger to a broom handle. This makes a good 'sweeper' to collect creatures from long vegetation.

– place a large white sheet on the ground under a likely bush. Gently shake the branches, and animals will fall on to the sheet.

**• find the conditions that woodlice prefer?**

Predictions can be made in the light of observations. Tests must be 'fair' and repeated for several different specimens before children can be sure. Try damp/ dry, light/ dark, smooth/ rough conditions. How many variables should be changed at a time? What is the effect of a change in temperature? What does the animal eat? How does it feed?

**Unit........................ Date........................**

# Teaching

**Have the children been provided with opportunities to:**

- work on questions or problems which they have accepted as their own? ☐
- develop their skills of exploration and investigation? ☐

See AT 1 evaluation checklist (page 11).

**Has the work children were engaged in allowed them to:**

PS 2
- explore and investigate at least two different localities and the ways in which plants and animals are suited to their location? ☐
- explore some ways in which plant behaviour and life cycles are influenced by:
  - – environmental conditions? ☐
  - – seasonal changes? ☐
  - – daily changes? ☐
  - – predator/prey relationships? ☐
- develop skills in:
  - – identifying locally occurring species of plants and animals, marking these against keys, using observable structural features of organisms :
  - – at first hand? ☐
  - – through sources provided by the teacher? ☐
  - – with increasing independence in the use of sources? ☐
  - – with developing awareness and understanding of the necessity for sensitive collection? ☐
- care for living things used as the subject of any study of the environment? ☐

PS 3
- investigate the effects of physical factors on the rate of plant growth, for example:
  - – light intensity? ☐
  - – temperature? ☐
  - – the amount of fertiliser? ☐

PS 4
- investigate and measure the similarities and differences between accessible:
  - – plants? ☐
  - – animals? ☐
- give attention to the welfare and protection of living material? ☐

PS 5
- study aspects of their local environment which have been affected by human activity? ☐

PS 9
- be aware of local distribution of some types of natural materials such as:
  - – sands? ☐
  - – soils? ☐
  - – rocks? ☐
- observe, through urban or rural fieldwork, how weather affects natural materials, including plants, in their surroundings, and how soil develops? ☐

**Unit .......... Date ..........**

# Learning

**Using investigations based on this unit, have the children demonstrated that they:**

**Level 1**

AT 3 • (can) name or label the external parts of plants? ☐

**Level 2**

AT 2 • know that plants and animals need certain conditions to sustain life? ☐

AT 3 • know that living things reproduce their own kind? ☐

AT 5 • (can) keep a diary, in a variety of forms, of change over time? ☐

**Level 3**

AT 2 • (can) recognise similarities and differences among living things? ☐

• can sort living things into broad groups according to observable features? ☐

• know that living things respond to seasonal and daily changes? ☐

AT 5 • know that human activity may produce local changes in the Earth's surface, air and water? ☐

AT 6 • know that some materials occur naturally while many are made from raw materials? ☐

AT 9 • understand how weathering of rocks leads to the formation of different types of soil? ☐

**Level 4**

AT 2 • (can) recognise similarities and differences both within and between groups of plants? ☐

• understand the key factors in the process of decay:

– temperature? ☐

– microbes? ☐

– compactness? ☐

– moisture? ☐

– and how this (process) is important in the re-use of biological material in everyday life? ☐

AT 4 • (can) measure variations in living organisms? ☐

**Level 5**

AT 2 • understand that the differences in physical factors between localities, including differences in seasonal and daily changes, are reflected in the different species of plants found there? ☐

• (can) assign organisms to their major groups using keys and observable features? ☐

• (can) support their view about environmental issues concerned with the use of fertilisers in agriculture and horticulture, based on their practical experience? ☐

See AT 1 evaluation checklist (page 11).

# UNIT 8
# HOW ANIMALS WORK

## Opportunities for learning

Working from this unit, children will be developing their investigative skills and their knowledge and understanding of:

- the diversity and classification of past and present life forms
- the organisation of living things and the processes which characterise their survival and reproduction
- the relationships, energy flows, cycles of matter and human influences within ecosystems

For greater detail, refer to the evaluation checklist (teaching) at the end of this unit.

## Topics

| | |
|---|---|
| **OUR POND** | Predator / prey relationships |
| **THE SOIL** | Living things / animals found in the soil |
| **THE SEASONS** | Seasonal changes in animals, life cycles |
| **ANIMALS AND THEIR YOUNG** | Growth and reproduction |

## Cross-curricular links

| | |
|---|---|
| **ART** | Camouflage, warning signs |
| **MATHEMATICS** | Handling information:<br>link children's names to pets owned<br>Balancing ( making mobiles ) |
| **MUSIC** | The sound an animal makes; how this relates to its size and the way it makes it ( a bee's summer buzz, an elephant's roar ) |
| **P E** | Moving as animals do |
| **TECHNOLOGY** | Bird feeders, cages for temporary care |

## Classroom materials

The following *Nelson Science* materials support this unit:

**Picture Resource Book 1**

- p.20 – migration; (spot the bird!)

**Picture Resource Book 2**

- p.1, 12 – mammals with young

- p.9 – a fish
- p.10 – a Great Grey Owl with young; the owl is a predator
- p.11 – a reptile
- p.13 – the life cycle of an amphibian
- p.14 – a nocturnal mammal which eats mainly insects
- p.15 – a mammal (a rodent) which shows a strong response to the changing seasons
- p.16 – the life cycle of an insect (the Monarch butterfly)
- p.17 – a baby mammal in a zoo
- p.18 – a mammal, a carnivore and a predator

**Picture Resource Book 3**

- p.12, 17 – mammals of economic importance

**Science Explorers**

- **Carrying Out Surveys 1, 2 and 3**
- **Experimenting 1, 2 and 3**
- **Problem Solving 1, 2 and 3**

## Related units

### Units in the Teacher's Classroom Manual (Key Stage 2)

- Colour, mirrors, lenses and prisms – Unit 1
- The local environment and beyond – Unit 4
- Our bodies – Unit 5
- Living things in the local environment – Unit 7
- Movement, forces and energy – Unit 11
- Everyday materials – Unit 13

### Units in the Teacher's Classroom Manual (Key Stage 1)

- How to take care of animals – Unit 11
- How animal life varies – Unit 12
- Seasonal and daily changes in animals – Unit 13

## Resources and equipment

- nets
- cylindrical tins
- clear sheets of acetate paper
- containers
- fabric
- matchboxes
- elastic bands
- hand lenses
- an aquarium tank
- junior reference books on the internal organs and organ systems of mammals

## Safety

Ensure that the children:

- pay attention to the welfare of living things at all times
- are not forced to participate in investigations if they have genuine phobias or cultural objections
- use only fresh hearts, lights, livers and kidneys; these should be disposed of on the same day, and anything that has contacted them (hands, trays, pencils, knives) should be thoroughly washed afterwards.

## Starting points

### The school environment

- a class pet
- animals in the school grounds
- teeth coming out; a collection of teeth
- a school birdtable
- a visit from a beekeeper

### The social environment

- pets, especially if they have produced / are producing young!
- a shell collection
- local animal sanctuaries
- family membership of the RSPCA, the RSPB or local volunteer conservation groups

### Further afield

- a visit to a zoo, a children's farm, a butterfly centre, a natural history museum, an urban farm, an environmental centre
- a visit to the seashore or other habitat

Also see 'Making connections'.

## Asking questions

### I wonder whether ...

- **the way an animal moves relates to the life it leads?**
- **every living creature is in danger of being eaten by another?**
- **we can tell what an animal eats from its teeth?**
- **the shape of a shell tells us how and where an animal lives?**
- **cold-blooded animals feel cold?**
- **it takes as long for a mother mouse to grow a baby as it takes a mother elephant?**
- **a honey-bee can go back to any hive?**

### What happens if ...

- **a stick insect needs to grow?**

## Gathering information

### Carrying out surveys

**Collecting information about:**

- **how some creatures need to move very fast, others roll up in a ball and put up defences, and others imitate their surroundings**
- **predator/ prey relationships**
- **the different shapes of their own teeth; link to dentition in herbivores, for example sheep, and carnivores, for example dogs**
- **shells shaped like suction pads, as opposed to screw-shaped shells which can 'drill' down into sand; make predictions about shells that are seen for the first time**
- **the fact that *cold-blooded* simply means that the animal cannot regulate its own body heat and may be quite hot if its surroundings are hot**
- **the fact that in mammals the baby develops inside the mother's body**
- **the communal nature of the life of a honey-bee**

### Experimenting

**Children:**

- **will discover the discarded skin of the insect, leading to a consideration of how animals without skeletons support themselves**

## Asking questions

### Can I find a way to ...

- **make a key to help someone else identify an animal?**
- **show that pond-snails always produce baby pond-snails?**
- **attract a greater variety of birds into the school grounds?**
- **move like a snake?**
- **make an easily cleaned cage for our stick insects?**
- **show how fossils might have been formed?**
- **see a real heart or real lungs?**

## Gathering information

### Solving practical problems

**Children:**

- **construct questions to help 'find' a fly when you have a worm, a snail, a spider and a fly**
- **observe the reproduction of the pond-snail or any other creature which can be kept in the classroom but can look after itself during half-term holidays**
- **discuss a variety of different designs for a bird feeder**
- **stand barefoot on a smooth, flat surface and move by wiggling the muscles in their toes in sequence**
- **take account of the need of the food plant for light and water**
- **imprint shells or leaves in plasticine by applying pressure and fill the imprints with plaster of Paris to make permanent records**
- **need to understand that if actual (sheep's) organs are going to be investigated, this is one occasion when they will not be allowed hands-on experience**

Examples of ways in which these ideas have been developed in the classroom are provided on pages 114–119.

## Handling information

- Encourage systematic listing and recording of data:
  - frequency tables
  - bar charts

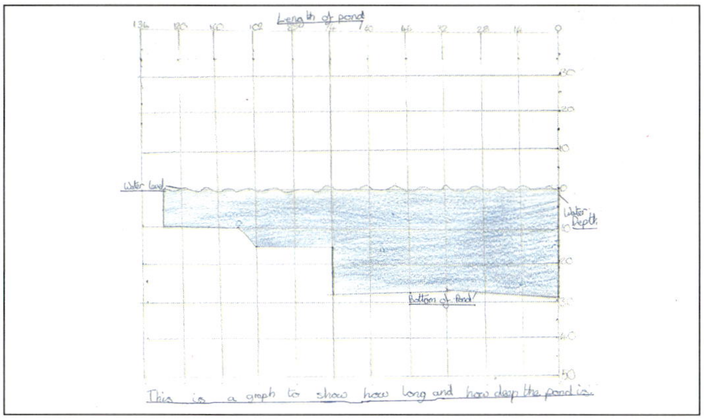


- Encourage searching for patterns in data.
- Encourage written and/or oral reporting skills as appropriate.
- Encourage the use of a limited technical vocabulary in communicating findings and ideas.

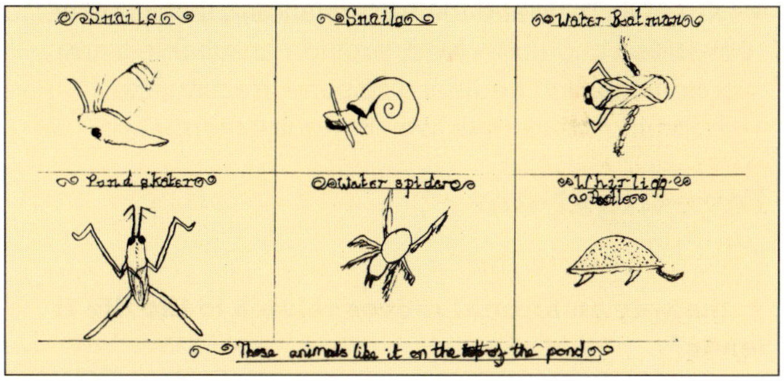


- Encourage the interpretation of data, and evaluation against the demands of the problem.

## Review points

The following are useful talking points:

### Our investigations

- new vocabulary we learned; for example: *similarities, differences, feature, information, life cycle, maintenance, process, digestion, environmental, herbivore, carnivore, genes, genetic, hereditary, circulation, mating, reproduction, reproduce, male, female, extinction, predator, prey, function, cell, organ, organism, soluble, relationship, generation, gestation, heart, liver, kidney, lung, blood vessel*; can we add to our definitions?
- the questions we raised that we answered, and those we must leave unanswered
- the variables we controlled, and those we should have or would like to have controlled
- the new equipment we used, or skills we learned; were we successful? do we need more practice?
- any patterns we noticed in the data or tentative hypotheses we made

### Making connections

- discuss the terms *animal* and *mammal* which are often confused
- the economic importance of honey-bees and the fact that they won't sting unless interfered with
- care of animals and the understanding that it is cruel to overfeed and underfeed, provide unsuitable living conditions, and neglect discipline, training and grooming for animals which require them

## Investigations

### I wonder whether ...

**• the way an animal moves relates to the life it leads?**

Discuss the link between movement and survival. Why does a hedgehog have short, stubby legs? How has this animal been disadvantaged by the invention of the motor car? Does a cat move differently when it's stalking its prey from the way it moves when escaping from a dog?

**• every living creature is in danger of being eaten by another?**

This investigation may lead to the drawing of food chains and then webs. This provides a link to Unit 5, 'Our bodies', and to cultural taboos about food; we eat eels and prawns in this country, but find odd the eating of termites in Africa, snakes in China and snails in France.

**• we can tell what an animal eats from its teeth?**

Use real animal teeth or skulls if available. This investigation may lead to finding out about the purpose of chewing and mixing food with the first digestive juice (saliva).

Ruminants have flat, grinding teeth and multiple stomachs to help them digest vegetation.

The connection between knife-like incisors and a diet of meat may also be made. This could be extended to the beak shape of predator birds.

**• the shape of a shell tells us how and where an animal lives?**

For example, the screw-shaped tower shell lives in sand, and if dislodged it will swivel round in a circle. The slipper limpet clings on to the rock, and the periwinkle shelters in cracks.

Children may wonder how animals can live in sand where there appears to be nothing to eat. This could lead to an investigation of filter feeders.

• **cold-blooded animals feel cold?**

Children could find out about reptiles, especially those with inflatable 'solar panels' on their backs to enable them to be active more quickly. Without the sun's heat their bodies are very sluggish.

• **it takes as long for a mother mouse to grow a baby as it takes a mother elephant?**

Children could find out about the aftercare which mammals provide for their young which are usually born fairly helpless and dependent on the mother's milk. Depending on school policy for sex education, this investigation may lead to a consideration of the mammalian reproductive system, including internal fertilisation of the egg.

- **a honey-bee can go back to any hive?**

An investigation of the design of the hive may be appropriate; how has hive design developed to make a colony of bees more manageable and to cause them least disturbance? The modern hive takes account of the relative sizes of the three types of bee (Queen, worker and drone) to keep the grubs out of the honey. The smell of a particular hive would prevent a bee from another colony being accepted.

## What happens if …

- **a stick insect needs to grow?**

Stick insects are easy to keep, and their behaviour, movement, growth and reproduction may be observed, drawn, measured and graphed.

## Can I find a way to …

- **make a key to help someone else identify an animal?**

- **show that pond-snails always produce baby pond-snails?**

A tank containing only pond-snails may be set up. Children may think that the eggs in their jelly have something to do with the plant life and this will have to be discussed.

Children should understand that if animals belong to the same species they can mate with each other and produce young.

- **attract a greater variety of birds into the school grounds?**

If a bird table is already available as a starting point, children could investigate the foods preferred by different species. If there is no bird table, a variety of feeders can be designed, using for example wire peanut holders, coconut halves, perches and plastic bottles.

Which kind of feeder does each species prefer? Does this relate to the shape of their beaks, their overall size or the shape of their feet?

Children could keep a diary recording the number of species, the time of day when they visit and their behaviour, including their behaviour towards other species and their flight patterns.

The investigation may be extended to find out about the visitors' preferred habitats, the shape, size, colour and number of eggs laid, their life cycles and their calls.

- **move like a snake?**

A snake moves by pushing its body from one side to another against pebbles and plants.

Expand to 'move like a cat' and so on.

- **make an easily cleaned cage for our stick insects?**
- **show how fossils might have been formed?**

Try 'preserving' animal tracks using plaster of Paris. Find out about insects in amber from secondary sources.

- **see a real heart or real lungs?**

Ask the abattoir staff to ensure that the vessels to and from the organs are not removed as they would be for consumption.

This work may be linked to Unit 5 'Our bodies', especially if you are using a heart with fat around it. Use models for preliminary explanations; even if they have to be borrowed from a secondary school, they are more effective than diagrams. Kidneys and livers may also be studied.

**Unit ........................ Date .........................**

# Teaching

**Have the children been provided with opportunities to:**

- work on questions or problems which they have accepted as their own? ☐
- develop their skills of exploration and investigation? ☐

See AT 1 evaluation checklist (page 11).

**Has the work pupils were engaged in allowed them to:**

PS 3
- investigate some aspects of feeding, support, movement and behaviour in relation to themselves and other animals? ☐
- be introduced to the functions of the major organ systems and to basic ideas about the processes of breathing, circulation, growth and reproduction? ☐

PS 4
- investigate and measure the similarities and differences between themselves and selected plants and animals (and their fossil counterparts)? ☐
- extend the study to cover extinct life forms and to include basic ideas about genetic and environmental influences? ☐
- give attention to the welfare and protection of living material? ☐

PS 2
- use secondary sources and, if possible, specimens, to explore the range of extinct life forms preserved as fossils? ☐

**Unit ........................** **Date ........................**

## Learning

**Using investigations based on this unit, have the children demonstrated that they:**

**Level 1**

AT2
- know that there is a wide variety of living things, which includes human beings?

**Level 2**

AT 2
- know that plants and animals need certain conditions to sustain life?
- understand how living things are looked after and (can) treat them with care and consideration?

AT 3
- know that living things reproduce their own kind?

**Level 3**

AT 2
- (can) recognise similarities and differences among living things?
- (can) sort living things into broad groups according to observable features?
- know that living things respond to seasonal and daily changes?

AT 3
- know that basic life processes: feeding, breathing, movement and behaviour, are common to human beings and the other living things they have studied?

**Level 4**

AT 2
- (can) recognise similarities and differences both within and between groups of animals?
- understand that animals can be preserved as fossils in different ways?

AT 3
- (can) name the major organs and organ systems in mammals?
- know about the factors which contribute to good health and body maintenance?
- understand the process of reproduction in mammals?

AT 4
- can measure variations in living organisms?

**Level 5**

AT 2
- (can) assign organisms to their major groups using keys and observable features?
- understand predator/prey relationships?

AT 3
- know that living things are made up from different kinds of cells which carry out different jobs?
- know that in digestion food is made soluble so that it can enter the blood?
- (can) describe the functions of the major organ systems?

AT 4
- know that information in the form of genes is passed on from one generation to the next?

See AT 1 evaluation checklist (page11).

# UNIT 9
# MEASURING THE WEATHER

## Opportunities for learning

Working from this unit, children will be developing their investigative skills and their knowledge and understanding of:

- the atmosphere and its changes over time
- information transfer

For greater detail, refer to the evaluation checklist (teaching) at the end of this unit.

## Topics

| | |
|---|---|
| **OUR SCHOOL** | Buildings |
| **CHILDREN IN OTHER COUNTRIES** | Clothes in different climates<br>Transport in different climates |
| **WATER** | Our water supply / the water cycle |

## Cross-curricular links

| | |
|---|---|
| **ART** | Six-pointed stars representing snow crystals<br>Paintings of dramatic skies, rainbows |
| **ENGLISH** | Poems and stories about ice, rain, puddles |
| **GEOGRAPHY** | Cold north wind / warm south wind<br>Water availability and use<br>Recording the weather over time |
| **HISTORY / GEOGRAPHY** | Prevailing winds; trade winds<br>Children were once sewn into their underwear in winter<br>Children walking to school with their lump of coal to contribute to the fire |
| **MATHEMATICS** | Using negative numbers in context<br>Graphs, bar charts<br>Designing a weather vane (reflective symmetry)<br>Using *clockwise* and *anti-clockwise* appropriately<br>Describing wind direction from a weather vane |
| **R E** | Biblical references to drought, flood and famine |

## Classroom materials

The following *Nelson Science* materials support this unit:

**Picture Resource Book 1**

- cover – a rainbow
- p.4 – look at the shadows; where is the sun?
- p.4, 5, 12, 20, 21, 22 – different climatic conditions
- p.12, 13 – shadow lengths
- p.14, 15 – what time of day?
- p.18 – suggestions for meteorological symbols
- p.10, 19 – seasonal changes

**Picture Resource Book 3**

- cover – Stonehenge
- p.3, 14 – how can you tell the time of year?
- p.9 – what weather symbols would we use for these days?
- p.10, 12 – what time of day is it?
- p.17 – storm damage

**Science Explorers**

- **Carrying Out Surveys 1, 2 and 3**
- **Experimenting 1, 2 and 3**
- **Problem Solving 1, 2 and 3**

## Related units

### Units in the Teacher's Classroom Manual (Key Stage 2)

- The local environment and beyond – Unit 4
- Living things in the local environment — Unit 7
- Everyday materials – Unit 13

### Units in the Teacher's Classroom Manual (Key Stage 1)

- Changes in the weather and the effect of the weather – Unit 14
- Changes in temperature: hot and cold – Unit 16

## Resources and equipment

- a maximum/ minimum thermometer, an alcohol thermometer
- clear plastic bottles with a measuring cylinder to calibrate
- plastic bowls with a supply of hot and ice-cold water
- assorted small pots including yoghurt pots
- nails, hammer, wood, tape, string
- paper/card in a variety of thicknesses
- mechanisms to help things easily rotate in the wind, for example: knitting needles, biro tops, beads
- a broom handle
- a barometer, a light meter and a temperature probe would be useful but not essential

**Safety**

Ensure that the children:
- take care with delicate instruments such as thermometers and barometers
- take care with upright knitting needles
- take care when using heat sources
- do not use mercury thermometers

## Starting points

### The school environment

- bad weather conditions
- large cardboard sheets held up on windy and still days
- litter and/ or leaves which are always blown to one corner of the playground
- the effects of the weather on school buildings, from slowly acting change leading to the need for painting and maintenance to sudden damage
- newspaper cuttings giving reports of floods/ winds/ tidal waves pinned to a noticeboard with weather charts from newspapers and magazines
- raising money for refugees fleeing a natural disaster
- steamed-up windows; spills which disappear or dry up on their own; a fish tank which needs topping up periodically
- children sending for brochures from water authorities

### The social environment

- television weather reports and weather charts
- holidays or relatives abroad
- traditional weather predictors based on the fact that it is more likely to rain when humidity is high, for example: the catgut weather house, seaweed, pine cones, folklore or sayings about the weather, even arthritis playing up!
- thermometers of all kinds
- the effects of the weather on plants
- drying clothes, hairdriers, hot-air hand driers in public toilets, radiator humidifiers

### Further afield

- a visit to people who need weather information in order to do their job, for example: a weather centre, an airport, a coastguard station, a lawyer, a farm
- weather records for the area: who kept them?
- a visit to a water purification plant or the local radio weather unit

Also see 'Making connections'.

## Asking questions

### I wonder whether ...

- all newspaper/ television weather reports use the same symbols for sunny or cloudy weather?
- something which is felt but not seen can affect the weather?
- every school in the country is having a wet weather break today?
- some parts of the country are always rainier/ sunnier than others?
- it is colder in the classroom at night than during the day?
- we can predict the weather from the clouds?
- meteorologists can predict the weather?

### What happens if ...

- we trick the heat sensors in our hands?
- we hold a moving air detector over a hot radiator?
- we bring a very cold, dry surface into the classroom?

### Can I find a way to ...

- make an instrument to measure rainfall?
- make an instrument to measure wind speed?
- make an instrument to measure wind direction?

## Gathering information

### Carrying out surveys

**Collecting information about:**

- weather reports from a variety of printed sources
- the heat of the sun which is felt but not seen; how important is it?
- news; sending letters; tapes or telephone reports to other schools
- average rainfall and average sunshine statistics, and the predicted date of the last frost in the area (from secondary sources)
- the use of a maximum/ minimum thermometer
- the meaning of cloud formations observed over time
- meteorologists' methods; how can they make their comparisons fair?

### Experimenting

**Children:**

- use three bowls of water, hot, cold and warm, labelled clearly, and devise an experiment to show the need for something more reliable than the heat sensors in our hands to tell us how hot or cold things are
- design and make a detector, for example, a coiled paper snake, and observe its behaviour in certain positions above the radiator, or other convenient heat source
- use iced water in a clear plastic container; dry the surface

### Solving practical problems

**Children:**

- design and make a rain gauge, and devise some form of calibration
- design and make an anemometer or substitutes for the Beaufort indicators
- design and make a weather vane or a wind-sock

Examples of ways in which these ideas have been developed in the classroom are provided on pages 128–133.

## Handling information

- Encourage systematic listing and recording of data:
  - frequency tables
  - bar charts

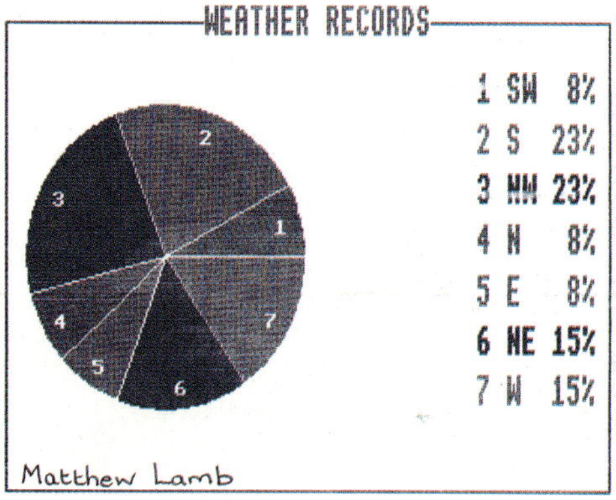


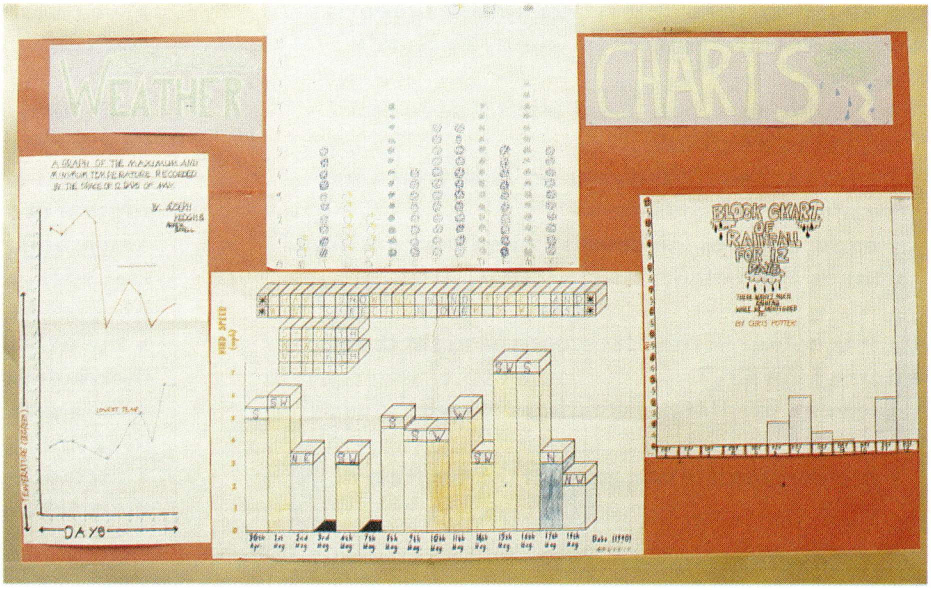


- Encourage searching for patterns in data.
- Encourage written and/or oral reporting skills as appropriate.

**Our Washing Day.**

Ria got a dolly punch and Mrs Abel brought an old mangle. We took them outside.Some children had a go of the posser and some children had a turn with the dolly peg. We had some shirts and aprons to wash. All the water came out when we put them through the mangle rollers. When we had done the washing we went back into school. It was hard work but it was fun.

By Laura Halpin

- Encourage the use of a limited technical vocabulary in communicating findings and ideas.
- Encourage the interpretation of data, and evaluation against the demands of the problem.

## Review points

The following are useful talking points:

### Our investigations

- new vocabulary we learned; for example: *meteorologist, wind-sock, anemometer, rain gauge, barometer, weather vane, thermometer, drought, flood, storm, wind, refugee*
- the three major cloud types: *cirrus, cumulus, stratus*
- the water cycle and associated words, for example: *atmosphere, rain, cloud, humidity, water vapour, evaporation, condensation* ; can we add to our definitions?
- the questions we raised that we answered, and those we must leave unanswered
- the variables we controlled, and those we should have or would like to have controlled
- the new equipment we used, or skills we learned; were we successful? do we need more practice?
- any patterns we noticed in the data or tentative hypotheses we made

### Making connections

- the effects of weather on people's lives, for example: ways of travelling to school in different areas of the country and different parts of the world
- the casualties of extreme weather conditions, for example: refugees from natural disasters such as crop failures; transport disruptions
- designing buildings to take account of the weather: for example, bridge design must balance strength with low wind resistance; tower blocks must withstand high wind speeds
- air supplies carried by astronauts and sub-aqua divers
- hydrogen balloons; advertising zeppelins
- water diviners (dowsers)

## Investigations

### I wonder whether ...

- **all newspaper/ television weather reports use the same symbols for sunny or cloudy weather?**

- **something which is felt but not seen can affect the weather?**

Evidence can be collected that the heat of the sun 'works' all the time, not just on sunny days. For example, puddles dry up and washing dries; where does the water go?

Children could design an experiment to show the importance of the sun (heat) in helping to make water evaporate. For example, they could make puddles

and then draw and measure the shrinking perimeters at agreed times.

Fill identical containers with different amounts of water and predict which will empty first.

- **every school in the country is having a wet weather break today**

What is the best way to record the data?

- **some parts of the country are always rainier/ sunnier than others?**

Find out about the length of the growing season in different areas. Compare crops grown: apples or wheat, for example.

- **it is colder in the classroom at night than during the day?**

Children read a maximum/minimum thermometer to find the highest and lowest temperature recorded in a twenty-four hour period.

Will the direction in which the instrument is facing affect the results?

How will they make their readings fair?

For how long will they make recordings?

- **we can predict the weather from the clouds?**

Using secondary sources and their own observations, children may identify the three major types of cloud and the weather with which they are associated.

- **meteorologists can predict the weather?**

Meteorologists collect information at the same time every day to make a fair comparison with the previous day. The results are plotted and stored to make a weather picture.

Meteorological balloons and satellites can record conditions high up in the atmosphere.

### What happens if ...

- **we trick the heat sensors in our hands?**

Children work in groups of three. One child is blindfolded and puts his/her left hand in cold water for, say, ten seconds. (S)he then puts the same hand in the warm water. Is the second bowl hot or cold?

Try the same thing with the right hand.

Can the same hand give different messages about the same bowl?

Do we really need thermometers when we have our senses to guide us?

- **we hold a moving air detector over a hot radiator?**

Children predict the best available material for making their detectors, and the best spot in which to hold them for maximum effect.

Decorate the detectors and suspend them from the ceiling, but think about the possible fire hazard.

Consider that it is the movement of air caused by differences in temperature over the Earth's surface which brings variations in the weather.

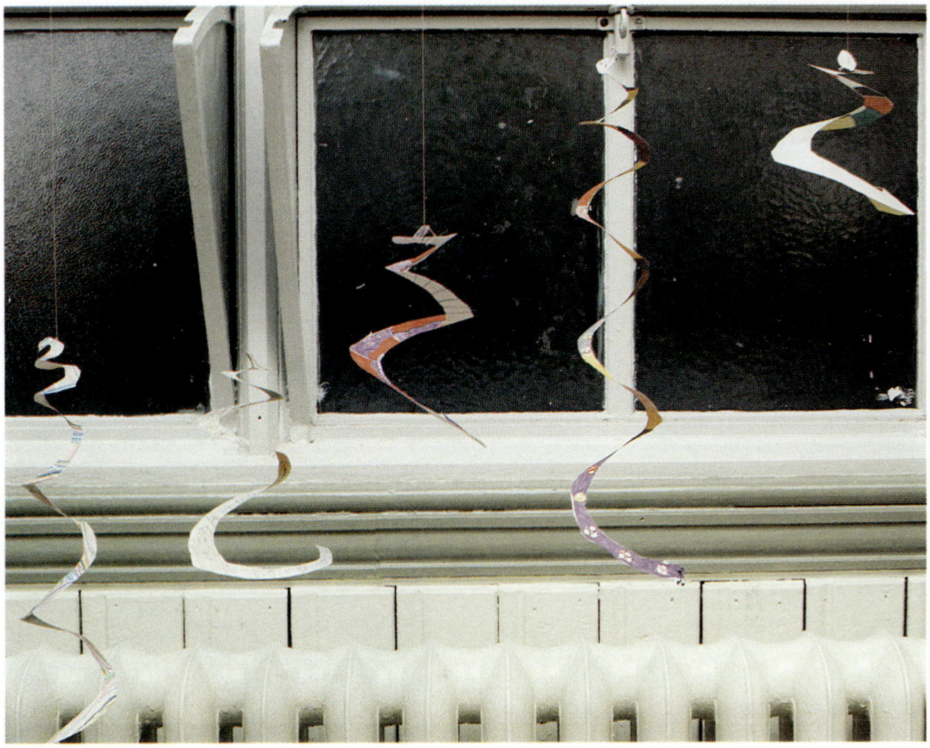

- **we bring a very cold, dry surface into the classroom?**

Children observe the condensation which forms on a surface and then consider where the water comes from. This helps them to understand what happens when the water vapour in a cloud drops as rain if it hits cold air.

### Can I find a way to ...

- **make an instrument to measure rainfall?**

Children design variations using a two-litre plastic lemonade bottle, sunk into the ground to prevent spillage.

Cut the top off the bottle where it begins to narrow, turn this funnel upside down and seal with tape.

Read and record every day using a measuring cylinder, or calibrate the gauge.

Children could develop the design to include a 'sleeve' for their gauge which will keep it clean and make it easier to remove for reading.

How else does water return to Earth? Consider the fact that snow, sleet and hail are all forms of water.

- **make an instrument to measure wind speed?**

To make an anemometer, use two identical lengths of wood (40 cm long) set at right angles to each other, with yoghurt pots fixed to the ends. Drill a hole in the centre of the cross, and insert a knitting needle capped by a biro top. Attach the needle to a post, and the device should rotate freely in the wind.

Calibrate using the Beaufort wind scale (0-12).

(A suspended protractor can record the angle at which a light object is blown by the wind.)

Children can make their own Beaufort scale using tissue and thick paper or card graded by weight and suspended over a bar or a broom handle.

Fix the scale if possible, or take a reading at certain fixed times of the day.

Example: Wind strength today: moved lightest tissue only.

This can be extended to using tissue paper on sticks as draught finders, to link with energy saving.

- **make an instrument to measure wind direction?**

Children could design a large cardboard arrow with a biro top fixed vertically at its mid-point.

Place the arrow on a knitting needle strapped to a post so that it can rotate freely.

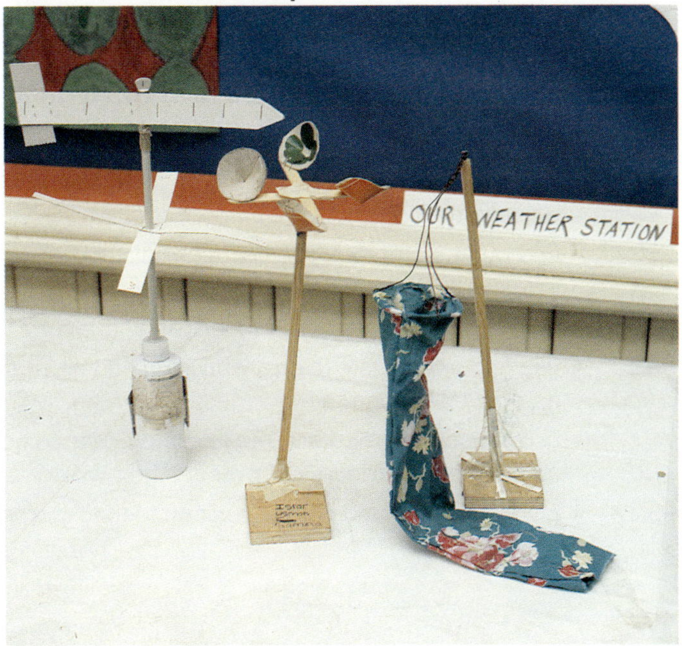

# Evaluation Checklist

**Unit** ........................ **Date** ........................

## Teaching

**Have the children been provided with opportunities to:**

- work on questions or problems which they have accepted as their own?
- develop their skills of exploration and investigation?

See AT 1 evaluation checklist (page 11).

**Has the work pupils were engaged in allowed them to:**

PS 9
- observe and make records of the weather and the seasons:
  - – regularly?
  - – qualitatively?

PS6
- find out the common uses of materials and relate their use to the properties they have investigated, such as changes brought about by heating and cooling?
- learn about the dangers associated with everyday materials?

PS 12
- use and investigate the transmission and storage of information using sensors, computers and the telephone?
- use sensors, computers, the telephone, tape recorders and digital watches in experiments and to store, retrieve and present their work?

PS 13
- investigate hot and cold in relation to their body temperature?

**Unit** ........................ **Date** ........................

## Learning

**Using investigations based on this unit, have the children demonstrated that they:**

**Level 1**

AT 9 • know that there is a variety of weather conditions? ☐
• (can) describe changes in the weather? ☐

AT 12 • know about some everyday devices which receive text, sound and images over long distances, using information technology? ☐

AT 16 • (can) describe through talking, or other appropriate means, the seasonal changes that occur in the weather and in living things? ☐
• know the danger of looking directly at the sun? ☐

**Level 2**

AT 9 • know that there are patterns in the weather which are related to seasonal changes? ☐
• know that the weather has a powerful effect on people's lives? ☐
• (can) record the weather over a period of time, in words, drawings and charts or other forms of communication? ☐

AT 12 • know that there is a variety of means for communicating information over long distances? ☐
• know that information can be stored using a range of everyday devices, including the computer? ☐

AT 13 • understand the meaning of hot and cold relative to the temperature of their own bodies? ☐

AT 6 • know that heating and cooling materials can cause them to melt or solidify or change permanently? ☐

**Level 3**

AT 9 • (can) describe from their observations some of the effects of weathering on buildings? ☐
– and on the landscape? ☐
• know that air is all around us? ☐
• (can) understand and interpret common meteorological symbols as used in the media? ☐

AT 13 • know that the temperature is a measure of how hot (or cold) things are? ☐

AT 16 • know that the inclination of the sun in the sky changes during the year? ☐

**Level 4**

AT 9 • (can) measure temperature? ☐
– rainfall? ☐
– wind speed? ☐
– (wind) direction? ☐
– (can) explain that wind is air in motion? ☐
• know that climate determines the success of agriculture? ☐
– and understand the impact of occasional catastrophic events? ☐

AT 12 • (can) detect and measure environmental changes using a variety of instruments? ☐

AT 13 • (can) measure temperature using a thermometer? ☐

AT 6 • understand the sequence of changes of state that results from heating or cooling? ☐
• (can) classify materials into solids, liquids and gases on the basis of their properties? ☐

**Level 5**

AT 9 • know that landscapes are formed by a number of agents including:
– weathering? ☐
– erosion? ☐
– and that these act over different time scales? ☐
• (can) explain the water cycle? ☐

AT 13 • understand the idea of global energy resources and appreciate that these resources are limited? ☐

AT 6 • know that gases have `weight'? ☐

See AT 1 evaluation checklist (page 11).

# UNIT 10
# OUR SOLAR SYSTEM

## Opportunities for learning

Working from this unit, children will be developing their investigative skills and their knowledge and understanding of:

- the relative positions and movement of the Earth, moon, sun and solar system within the universe

For greater detail, refer to the evaluation checklist (teaching) at the end of this unit.

## Topics

| | |
|---|---|
| **ENERGY** | The sun |
| **SPACE TRAVEL** | Weightlessness<br>Minerals brought back to Earth from space |
| **FAMOUS PEOPLE** | Copernicus, Kepler, Galileo, Newton |
| **MYTHS AND LEGENDS** | Flat Earth<br>Greek and Roman gods |

## Cross-curricular links

| | |
|---|---|
| **ART** | The creation of the universe |
| **DRAMA** | Costumes representing seasons |
| **ENGLISH** | Science fiction |
| **GEOGRAPHY** | Time zones<br>Physical geography |
| **HISTORY** | The development of scientific ideas |
| **MATHEMATICS** | Size and scale |
| **TECHNOLOGY** | Creating an 'environment', for example a fantasy moonscape |

## Classroom materials

The following *Nelson Science* materials support this unit:

**Picture Resource Book 1**

- p.15 - the moon, showing surface shading
- p.16 - four of the planets in our solar system showing their relationships with each other (orbits) but *not* their scale or the distances between them

**Science Explorers**

- **Carrying Out Surveys 1, 2 and 3**
- **Experimenting 1, 2 and 3**
- **Problem Solving 1, 2 and 3**

## Related units

### Units in the Teacher's Classroom Manual (Key Stage 2)

- Colour, mirrors, lenses and prisms – Unit 1
- The local environment and beyond – Unit 4
- Living things in the local environment – Unit 7
- Measuring the weather – Unit 9

### Units in the Teacher's Classroom Manual (Key Stage 1)

- Seasonal and daily changes in animals – Unit 13
- Changes in the sky: light and dark – Unit 15

## Resources and equipment

- a globe
- a torch
- an overhead projector
- a beach ball, a pea, a white ball of tennis ball size
- a darkened area
- small plastic figures, such as those from Christmas crackers
- reference books and science fiction books

### Safety

Ensure that the children:

- never look directly at the sun, or other strong light sources used in these investigations
- avoid looking at a full moon through binoculars or a telescope

## Starting points

### The school environment

- a sunny day
- sunglasses
- an eclipse of the sun
- a globe
- the Star of Bethlehem at Christmas
- videos of space missions

### The social environment

- camping in the countryside, and seeing the stars without any light pollution
- media reports of the space programme
- films and television programmes, magazines, books and computer games depicting space travel
- holiday travel or friends and relatives living in other climates and time zones

### Further afield

- a visit to a planetarium, Greenwich (the zero meridian) or Jodrell Bank
- a visit to a museum to see an astrolabe, an orrery, a sun-dial

Also see 'Making connections'.

## Asking questions

### I wonder whether ...

- there are places in the world where it is night while we are having day?
- the moon changes in the same way every month?
- I can draw the sun, the moon and the Earth to scale
- mankind has always known that the sun is at the centre of our solar system?
- our sun is a star?

### What happens if ...

- I spin round while wearing a circular skirt?
- the Earth, the moon and the sun are in a straight line, with the Earth or moon blocking the sun?

### Can I find a way to ...

- tell the time using the sun?
- make a model to show day and night?
- make a model of our solar system?
- show the way in which light is reflected off the moon's surface?
- show why we have seasons, using a model?

## Gathering information

### Carrying out surveys

**Children:**

- find out about time zones
- design a recording system to show how the moon changes, and then look for patterns in the results
- find out the distances between the planets from secondary sources, and then work out a scale
- find out from secondary sources about the lives of some of the first astronomers
- find out what causes the stars to twinkle

### Experimenting

**Children:**

- think about things which can spin and what happens if they are let go
- children predict, then use models or drawings to try to find an answer

### Solving practical problems

**Children:**

- find something which makes a clear shadow, and then devise a method to hold it still for an extended period
- may devise a model before finding out about time zones (above), and deduce that they are necessary
- collect or make objects which are roughly to scale for the planets within our solar system, but accept that distances are impossible to represent
- investigate the way the shadows of round objects form, using a strong, stationary light source, and link their observations to their recordings of the changing shape of the moon (see above)
- need to understand the angle of the Earth's axis when it orbits the sun

Examples of ways in which these ideas have been developed in the classroom are provided on pages 140–143.

## Handling information

- Encourage systematic listing and recording of data:
  - frequency tables
  - bar charts
- Encourage searching for patterns in data.
- Encourage written and/or oral reporting skills as appropriate.
- Encourage the use of a limited technical vocabulary in communicating findings and ideas.

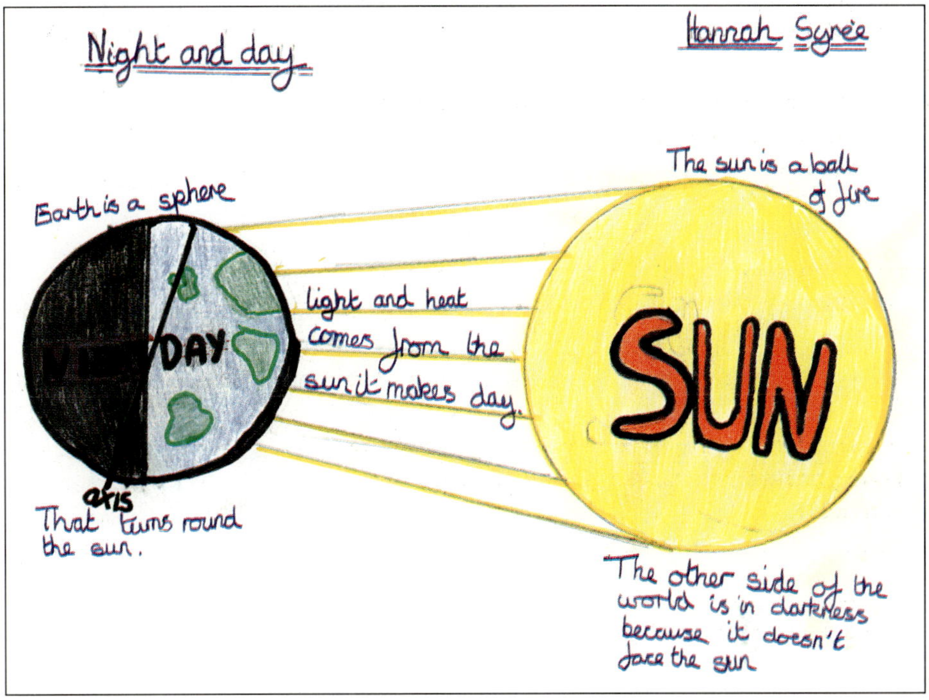


- Encourage the interpretation of data, and evaluation against the demands of the problem.

> "It is impossible to draw the space between the sun and earth to scale. The page would have to be as big as the playground.

## Review points

The following are useful talking points:

### Our investigations

- new vocabulary we learned; for example: *clockwise, anti-clockwise, sphere, spherical, new moon, full moon, crescent moon, surface, crater, solar system, axis, constellation, spinning, centrifugal force, eclipse, moonlight, light year, orbit, comet, telescope, gravity, space, heresy, astronomy, geometry, planet, planetarium, 'heavenly body', vacuum, star, galaxy, universe, weightlessness, volcano, erupt, molten, lava*; can we add to our definitions?
- the questions we raised that we answered, and those we must leave unanswered

- the variables we controlled, and those we should have or would like to have controlled
- the new equipment we used, or skills we learned; were we successful? do we need more practice?
- any patterns we noticed in the data or tentative hypotheses we made

### Making connections

- Stonehenge, completed 4,000 years ago, which is believed to have been built as a means of keeping track of the seasons through the movement of the sun
- famous large telescopes
- the discovery in the 1930s of radio telescopes which can trace unseen stars by means of radio waves; we now know that there are billions of other galaxies beyond the Milky Way
- fossils; volcanoes
- comets, meteors and craters
- navigation by the stars
- identifying constellations of stars
- fairground rides (based on centrifugal force)
- honey extractors which use centrifugal force to remove the liquid honey from the wax comb
- the difference between weight and mass

## Investigations

### I wonder whether ...

**• there are places in the world where it is night while we are having day?**

This survey could draw on a variety of personal experiences, as well as secondary sources.

**• the moon changes in the same way every month?**

This investigation is best done in the autumn or winter when it gets dark before bed-time.

Observations can take place over an extended period to allow for a pattern to emerge despite missed readings due to cloud and other factors.

**• I can draw the sun, the moon and the Earth to scale?**

If the sun is represented by a beach ball, the Earth on the same scale is the size of a pea. The distance between ball and pea should be about 35 metres. Children will probably need to go into the playground to measure this distance. Depending on the size of the sheet of paper, it may be possible to draw only a small part of the sun if all the planets are drawn to the same scale. Don't even attempt to represent the distance between them.

This may be an appropriate time to reflect that a year is our measure of the $365\frac{1}{4}$ days it takes for the Earth (pea) to travel round the sun (beach ball).

**• mankind has always known that the sun is at the centre of our solar system?**

Children could find out about the first astronomers: Kepler, Galileo, Newton.

**• our sun is a star?**

Children could find out from secondary sources that stars are huge spheres of

gas, glowing with the extreme heat of internal nuclear fission. The light is a by-product of the heat; a comparison could be the glowing of an electric cooker ring.

All the stars that can be seen with the naked eye belong to our galaxy, the Milky Way, a spiral shape made of huge numbers of stars (a hundred thousand million at the last count).

### What happens if ...

- **I spin round while wearing a circular skirt?**

Children can observe that the effect of spinning round is to fling the edges of the skirt as far away from the central point as possible. Similarly, if a child is spun round by an adult, the adult has to lean back to compensate for this outward pull.

Gravity is an important factor in explaining the moon's orbit around the Earth. The moon does not float out into space because this outward pull is balanced by gravity's inward pull.

- **the Earth, the moon and the sun are in a straight line, with the Earth or moon blocking the sun?**

Children may construct models to investigate this problem, or, if they understand about light travelling in straight lines, they may be able to draw rays to explain the eclipse of the moon or the eclipse of the sun, depending on their relative positions.

### Can I find a way to ...

- **tell the time using the sun?**

Children could make a shadow-stick or sun-dial from a piece of dowelling held in a cotton reel. Fix the dowelling firmly in the middle of a board, and mark the shadow at hourly intervals, using a compass to mark north/ south/ east/ west.

See Unit 15 in the *Teacher's Classroom Manual (Key Stage 1).*

Use the record to:

– predict the time on the classroom clock at intervals on the following day

– predict the results of readings three months later

– compare the two sets of results

Children could consider how to make these observations 'fair'. (For example, the stick must be kept in the same position.)

Why are winter shadows longer than summer ones?

- **make a model to show day and night?**

Using a torch or light from an overhead projector to represent the light from the sun, children illuminate one side of a globe. By turning the globe slowly anti-clockwise while keeping the light source stationary, they can watch day turn through dusk into night. Fasten small plastic figures to the British Isles and to other countries known to the children and ask directed questions, for example, who goes to bed first? Use card if the figures need to be flexible; make them the same size in order to compare their shadows and relate this to the work on sun-dials.

**• make a model of our solar system?**

Children could find out about Mercury, Venus, Earth, Mars, Jupiter, Saturn, Uranus, Neptune and Pluto. They could then make nine round objects of the approximate relative sizes, label them and position them in the correct order in relation to the sun. Point out that it would be impossible to represent the distances to scale.

**• show the way in which light is reflected off the moon's surface?**

Children could plan an investigation to explain why the moon looks bright even though it generates no light of its own.

Working in a dark area and using a torch to represent the sun, they could place a football (the Earth) and a tennis ball (the moon) in the beam, moving the 'moon' round the 'Earth' and observing the light and shadows on the 'moon'.

**• show why we have seasons, using a model?**

To represent the Earth's passage around the sun, one child stands facing a model sun. Holding a globe with the North Pole facing the 'sun', i.e. away from the body (northern summer), (s)he then walks a 'do-si-do' (the country dancing step) right round the 'sun' in an anti-clockwise direction.

When the child's back is to the sun, the globe is said to be positioned at 'northern winter'; when the sun is at the right arm, 'northern spring', at the left arm, 'northern autumn'.

Once the children are used to this movement, the four key positions can be recorded, exchanging the model sun for a light source.

This not-quite-circular orbit takes $365\frac{1}{4}$ days; discuss the need for a Leap Year to make the calendar work.

This investigation can be extended by including the daily anti-clockwise rotation of the Earth on its axis. Children may observe the shadow cast by a figure fixed to the British Isles while the globe, in its summer position, is turned on its axis one full turn anti-clockwise.

If the same is done with the globe in its winter position, children may begin to understand seasonal differences in day length and in the position of the sun in the sky.

**Unit ........................** **Date ........................**

## Teaching

**Have the children been provided with opportunities to:**

- work on questions or problems which they have accepted as their own? ☐
- develop their skills of exploration and investigation? ☐

See AT 1 evaluation checklist (page 11).

**Has the work pupils were engaged in allowed them to:**

PS 16
- investigate changes in:
  - the night sky? ☐
  - the positions of the moon, through direct observations? ☐
  - and through secondary sources? ☐
- use a simple model of the solar system to attempt explanations of:
  - day and night? ☐
  - year length? ☐
  - changes in the aspect of the moon? ☐
  - changes in the elevation of the sun? ☐
- be introduced to the principle of the sun-dial as a means of noting the passage of time? ☐
- learn about the positions and movements of the Earth, moon and sun in relation to each other? ☐

PS 15
- carry out investigations on shadows? ☐

# Evaluation Checklist

**Unit ........................** **Date ........................**

## Learning

**Using investigations based on this unit, have the children demonstrated that they:**

**Level 1**

AT 16
- know the danger of looking directly at the sun? ☐
- (can) describe, in relation to their home or school, the apparent daily motion of the sun across the sky? ☐

AT 15
- know that light comes from different sources? ☐

**Level 2**

At 16
- (can) explain why night occurs? ☐

  know that:
- day length changes throughout the year? ☐
- we live on a large, spherical, self-contained planet, called Earth? ☐
- the Earth, moon and sun are separate bodies? ☐

AT 15
- know that light passes through some materials and not others, and that when it does not, shadows may be formed? ☐

**Level 3**

AT 16
- know that the inclination of the sun in the sky changes during the year? ☐
- (can) measure time with a sun-dial? ☐

**Level 4**

AT 16
- know that the phases of the moon change in a regular manner? ☐
  – and a predictable manner? ☐
- know that the solar system is made up of the sun and planets, and have an idea of its scale? ☐
- understand that the sun is a star? ☐

AT 15
- know that we see objects because light is scattered off them and into our eyes? ☐
- know that light travels in straight lines and use this to explain the shapes and sizes of shadows? ☐

**Level 5**

AT 16
- (can) relate a simple model of the solar system to day/night and year length? ☐
  – changes of day length? ☐
  – seasonal changes? ☐
  – and changes in the inclination of the sun? ☐
- (can) observe and record the shape and surface shading of the phases of the moon over a period of time? ☐

AT 15
- understand how light is reflected? ☐

See AT evaluation checklist (page 11).

# UNIT 11
# MOVEMENT, FORCES AND ENERGY

## Opportunities for learning

Working from this unit, children will be developing their investigative skills and their knowledge and understanding of:

- forces; their nature, their significance and their effects on the movement of objects
- the nature of energy; its transfer and control

For greater detail, refer to the evaluation checklist (teaching) at the end of this unit.

## Topics

| | |
|---|---|
| **FLIGHT** | Spinners, parachutes, aeroplanes |
| **TRANSPORT** | Wheels, friction, gears, road safety |
| **LEISURE** | Fairground rides, marinas |
| **WATER** | Movement on, in, over and because of water |
| **ENERGY** | Energy transfer / storage |

## Cross-curricular links

| | |
|---|---|
| **GEOGRAPHY** | Journeys; how and why people make them<br>Transport in mountainous regions / deserts<br>Road, rail, air and sea travel |
| **HISTORY** | The development of the wheel<br>The history of flight |
| **MATHEMATICS** | Measuring |
| **P E** | 'Test flights' in the playground; pushes and pulls<br>'Moving like' well known animals |
| **TECHNOLOGY** | Garages; traffic lights |

## Classroom materials

The following *Nelson Science* materials support this unit:

**Picture Resource Book 1**

- p.1 – 'parachutes'; characteristics of things which can be carried by wind
- p.17 – the force of the wind

**Picture Resource Book 2**

- p.3 – machines, wheels, movement and safety
- p.4, 5 – simple machines, chopsticks, knives and forks
- p.4, 6, 19 – complicated machines including wheels, caterpillar tracks, levers, slopes and pulleys; safety
- p.17 – a machine which makes work easier

**Science Explorers**

- **Carrying Out Surveys 1, 2 and 3**
- **Experimenting 1, 2 and 3**
- **Problem Solving 1, 2 and 3**

## Related units

### Units in the Teacher's Classroom Manual (Key Stage 2)

- Our bodies – Unit 5
- How flowering plants work – Unit 6
- How animals work – Unit 8
- Everyday materials – Unit 13

### Units in the Teacher's Classroom Manual (Key Stage 1)

- How to make things move – Unit 17

## Resources and equipment

- assorted toys, for example: cars, balloons, bubble mix and blowers, wind-up toys, a jack-in-the-box, springs
- a variety of paper and card, including corrugated card
- 'junk' such as clean polystyrene meat trays, toilet roll centres, washing-up liquid bottles, cottonreels, dowelling, lollipop sticks and matchsticks
- a long piece of string
- plasticine
- a collection of balls made of different materials and in different sizes
- paperclips
- elastic bands
- plastic containers
- syringes with plastic tubing
- coat-hangers and wire-cutters
- a glue gun
- a Newton meter

### Safety

Ensure that the children:

- only cut up items such as plastic bottles or wire if you consider they can safely do so; otherwise it should be done in advance

## Starting points

### The school environment

- the need for yellow zigzag lines outside the school gates
- cycling proficiency tests; a visit from the local Road Safety Officer
- a survey of the tyres on cars in the school car park
- the balls which are permitted in playtime
- doors, mobiles, balances
- a video from RNLI
- resources from RoSPA

### The social environment

- making paper darts and spinners, blowing bubbles, flying kites
- advertisements in newspapers, on hoardings and on television warning motorists of the need to wear seat belts and to allow for stopping distances
- road signs and markings which regulate traffic speed
- bicycle gearing; record how many times the back wheel turns for a complete turn on the chain
- sailing; cross-Channel ferries

### Further afield

- visits to a working wind- or water-wheel, an airport, the industrial machines in a science museum, a transport museum, a harbour, a fairground, a theme park, a natural history museum

Also see 'Making connections'.

## Asking questions

**I wonder whether …**

- **I can walk up a slope more easily than the others in my group?**
- **the sail of a yacht is always triangular?**
- **I can find a use for a lever?**
- **I can make something useful with a spring?**

## Gathering information

**Carrying out surveys**

**Children:**

- **make predictions, and then design a fair test for the grip on their shoes**
- **survey secondary sources to gather information about sail designs; can they make a sail which would work on land?**
- **find out what a lever is, and then find out how they are used by looking around the classroom and surveying secondary sources**
- **find out where springs are used in the classroom, for example: in a Newton meter, scales, a stapler, a coiled electric flex**

## Asking questions

### What happens if ...

- I stick a piece of plasticine to a ball before rolling it?
- I blow through a hole in the middle of a flat piece of card?
- we drop different kinds of ball on to the same surface?
- I pull out the tablecloth when there is something standing on it?
- I suddenly stop my toy vehicle when there is a model figure on the back?
- I put a rubber band round two cottonreels and then turn one clockwise?

### Can I find a way to ...

- move six books with my little finger?
- make a toy which is hard to knock over?
- make a crash barrier for my toy car?
- make something that spins better than a sycamore seed?
- make a model that moves using a rubber band?
- make a balloon-powered model?
- make a sheet of paper fly to the left?
- use water power to make my dumper truck tip?
- make a ball of plasticine float?

## Gathering information

### Experimenting

**Children:**

- predict and then experiment (on as flat a surface as possible)
- try pushing a piece of card across the floor, or flipping it by waving newspaper; is blowing down a hole in the centre more effective, especially on a rough surface?
- predict which will hit the surface first, or design an experiment to show the best bouncer; which variables need controlling?
- set up a can with a weight in the bottom on a tablecloth, and try to pull the cloth out without upsetting the can; is the weight crucial?
- run their car or pram with the model figure (unattached) down a slope to a low barrier or wall; observe the path (trajectory) made by the figure when it falls
- experiment with two, three or four labelled cottonreels nailed to a board, observing and recording the effects of joining them in different ways using a large rubber band

### Solving practical problems

**Children:**

- find out about the history of the wheel
- investigate balance; how do budgies' toys work?
- design a barrier which will crumple to absorb the forces, and stop the car without damaging it
- observe a sycamore seed closely and make spinners with two, three and four wings; which spins best? which comes back to you? why would this be a bad design for a sycamore seed?
- consider the problem of allowing the rubber band to unwind with the minimum of friction; try making tanks and other vehicles
- think about the means of attachment and whether their model is to move on land, in water or through the air
- design different kinds of dart
- make a simple 'lift and lower' truck, starting with a simple syringe hydraulic mechanism; the idea can be broadened to many other moving models
- make plasticine boats of different shapes but using the same amount of plasticine

Examples of ways in which these ideas have been developed in the classroom are provided on pages 153–159.

## Handling information

- Encourage systematic listing and recording of data:
  - frequency tables
  - bar charts

Name Jenny Bond Date 25.9.90

2. Pushing a brick on different surfaces.

| Kind of surface | Prediction | What happened? |
| --- | --- | --- |
| Sand | It will dig in I thik so | it did dig in but it was good and it slide to. |
| towel | I thik it will be very difficult | it was very difficult becuse the towel crinkle. up and it did slide. |
| soft fabric | I thik it will be difficlt but it will slide | it was very difficult becuse it crinkle up and it did slide. |
| Plastic | I thik it will slide very easy | it rolled over and it wast very good at all |
| carpet | I thik it will be easy but it will slide | it rolled over and it wast very good at all |
| corrugated card | I thik it will be difficll but it will slide | it crinkle. up and it did not move at all. |
| straw matting | I thik it will be difficll but it will slide | it did slide and it was good. |
| | | |

- Encourage searching for patterns in data.
- Encourage written and/or oral reporting skills as appropriate.

- Encourage the use of a limited technical vocabulary in communicating findings and ideas.
- Encourage the interpretation of data, and evaluation against the demands of the problem.

## Review points

The following are useful talking points:

### Our investigations

- new vocabulary we learned; for example: *force, weight, newton, transfer, energy, pivot, balance, fulcrum, float, sink, gears, belt, lever, cog*; can we add to our definitions?
- the questions we raised that we answered, and those we must leave unanswered
- the variables we controlled, and those we should have or would like to have controlled
- the new equipment we used, or skills we learned; were we successful? do we need more practice?
- any patterns we noticed in the data or tentative hypotheses we made

### Making connections

- a horse rider being thrown over the horse's head if it stops suddenly
- road safety advertisements demonstrating:

  – the need for seat belts, because car passengers keep moving if the car stops suddenly

  – the need for good tread on tyres, as friction is a useful force when grip is needed

  – the need to be aware of the relationship between stopping distance and miles per hour; the faster the vehicle is moving, the longer it takes to stop it

  – whiplash injuries and the advisability of head rests
- lorry escape routes on steep hills; they run into sand
- crash barriers; cars with 'crumple zones' to absorb impact
- hovercraft which work by forcing air downwards
- pulley systems (in cranes, at garages)
- cogs (on bicycles, switchback railways, merry-go-rounds)
- parachutes: their shape, how to control them, what they are made of
- the shape of a bird's wing, an aeroplane wing or a sail, for maximum 'lift'
- seesaws, wheelbarrows, bottle openers; all use fulcrums
- speculating about dropping a penny and a brick from a tower; which would hit the ground first?
- steam power; working models or full-sized traction engines, trains, funfair rides
- cargo ships; the compromise between their load-carrying capacity and the need to move through the water, the materials from which they are constructed, plimsoll lines
- energy sources of the future, for example wave power and solar power

## Investigations

### I wonder whether ...

- **I can walk up a slope more easily than the others in my group?**

Children could think about the surface and steepness of the slope, and the 'grip' (friction) of their shoes. When do we need good grip? When do we try to reduce grip?

- **the sail of a yacht is always triangular?**

Try making model land yachts with sails attached. Which shape works best? How do you make a 'fair' test?

- **I can find a use for a lever?**

Children may begin to classify their findings.

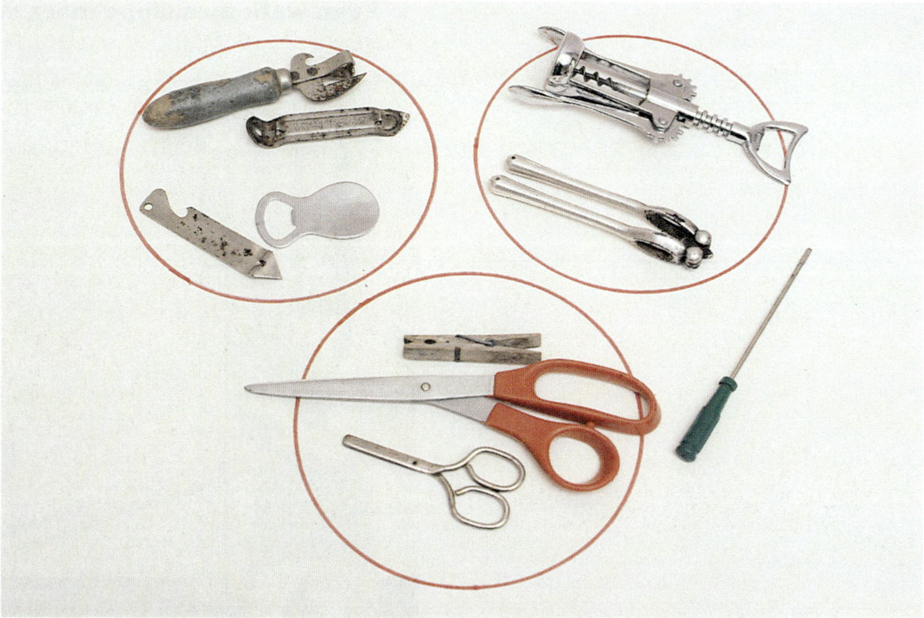

- **I can make something useful with a spring?**

Children could design and make a spring balance, but must understand about elastic limits and not overstretch the spring! They could try to make their own springs using wire tightly curled around a pen. Try making a jack-in-the-box or other toys from bought springs.

### What happens if ...

- **I stick a piece of plasticine to a ball before rolling it?**

Children reflect on the notion that the ball with the weight attached is deflected from its course just as surely as if there were a force acting on it.

- **I blow through a hole in the middle of a flat piece of card?**

Children investigate the principle of the hovercraft. Does the size of the hole affect the movement? Try the experiment using other materials such as a polystyrene meat tray. Which is best? Make it a fair test by using a hairdrier, or a balloon.

- **we drop different kinds of ball on to the same surface?**

Which variables can we keep the same? Does gravity work in the same way on all the balls?

- **I pull out the tablecloth when there is something standing on it?**

Children may experiment with (unbreakable!) items, and then develop magic tricks once they have understood the importance of the object's centre of gravity.

- **I suddenly stop my toy vehicle when there is a model figure on the back?**

Stopping the vehicle dead can be linked with the function of a crash barrier. Does the distance travelled by the figure link with the speed of the vehicle on impact?

- **I put a rubber band round two cottonreels and then turn one clockwise?**

Children make sure that the cottonreels turn freely and the band is not too tight. Experiment by substituting objects of different sizes for the cottonreels.

## Can I find a way to ...

- **move six books with my little finger?**

Try using pencils as 'logs'; using a shiny surface; making runners; making wheels from junk and attaching them to axles; using marbles.

- **make a toy which is hard to knock over?**

A ball of plasticine inside the lid of a coffee jar can demonstrate the principle of balancing toys. Decorated plastic eggs, with the bottom half weighted, work well.

- **make a crash barrier for my toy car?**

Children draw on their knowledge of the strength and elasticity of materials. Plasticine-fronted wood could be a starting point.

- **make something that spins better than a sycamore seed?**

How does the length and/or thickness of the wings affect the spin?

- **make a model that moves using a rubber band?**

Use a cottonreel, a washing-up liquid bottle or an aluminium can.

Children can make endless variations, adding different superstructures representing dragons, tanks and so on. Alternatively, stand the model on end to provide the base for a merry-go-round.

- **make a balloon-powered model?**

Children consider the factors which must be taken into account, such as the weight of the materials.

A rocket on a string, a hovercraft and a light wheeled vehicle are all effective.

- **make a sheet of paper fly to the left?**

Children could work out the factors which give maximum lift, the straightest flight and a circular flight. These factors will include the method of launching as well as the addition and subtraction of paperclips or plasticine weights.

- **use water power to make my dumper truck tip?**

Children could investigate the principles of hydraulics with the help of coloured water. Does the system work as well without the water? This investigation can be extended to a consideration of pneumatics.

- **make a ball of plasticine float?**

If the standard unit of load is something like a paperclip, make the plasticine balls about ten grams in weight. Which shape of boat will carry the most paperclips? Does the way the clips are positioned affect the result? Will the shape which carries the greatest load also be the fastest? How could the children test this aspect? Record the results.

**Unit ...................... Date .........**

# Teaching

**Have the children been provided with opportunities to:**

- work on questions or problems which they have accepted as their own? ☐
- develop their skills of exploration and investigation? ☐

See AT 1 evaluation checklist (page 11).

**Has the work pupils were engaged in allowed them to:**

PS 10
- experience different types of force? ☐
- use measurement to compare the effects of force in the context of, for example, bridge building? ☐
- investigate the forces involved in floating and sinking? ☐
- explore the forces involved in:
  - movement? ☐
  - friction? ☐
  - falling? ☐
- set the work in everyday contexts, for example:
  - road safety? ☐
  - transport, including cycling and sailing? ☐
  - balancing systems? ☐
  - hydraulic mechanisms as used in model making? ☐

PS 13
- investigate a variety of devices which are self-propelled and in which energy can be stored, for example:
  - rubber bands? ☐
  - springs? ☐
  - balloons? ☐

**Unit ........................** **Date ........................**

## Learning

**Using investigations based on this unit, have the children demonstrated that they:**

**Level 1**

AT 10 • know that things can be moved by pushing them? ☐

**Level 2**

AT 13 • (can) describe how a toy with a simple mechanism which moves and stores energy works? ☐

**Level 3**

AT 10 • understand that forces are acting on things when they:
- are changed in shape? ☐
- begin to move? ☐
- or stop moving? ☐

• understand the factors which cause objects to float or sink in water? ☐

AT 13 • understand, in qualitative terms, that models and machines need a source of energy in order to work? ☐

• (can) use simple power sources (rubber bands)? ☐
- and devices which transfer energy (gears, belts, levers)? ☐

**Level 4**

AT 10 • understand that the movement of an object depends on the size and direction of the forces exerted on it, for example, in the context of investigations with:
- elastic-powered models? ☐
- and wind-powered models? ☐

• understand that the greater the speed of an object the greater the force and/or the time that is needed to stop it? ☐
- and understand the significance of this for road safety? ☐

• understand that things fall because of a force of attraction towards the centre of the Earth? ☐

• (can) recognise that weight is a force? ☐
- and know that it is measured in newtons? ☐

AT 13 • understand that energy can be stored, and transferred to and from moving things? ☐

**Level 5**

AT 10 • understand that when an object is not moving relative to its environment ... ☐
- or when it is moving at a steady speed without change of direction ... ☐
- there are balanced forces acting upon it, for example, a car standing at rest on the surface of the Earth?

• (can) measure:
- forces? ☐
- distance? ☐
- and time? ☐

• (can) describe the effect of friction on moving objects? ☐

See AT 1 evaluation checklist (page 11).

# UNIT 12
# WEATHERING, MINERALS, ROCKS AND SOIL

## Opportunities for learning

Working from this unit, children will be developing their investigative skills and their knowledge and understanding of:

- the properties of materials, and the way in which these determine the uses of the materials and form the basis of their classification
- the structure and main features of the Earth and its change over time

For greater detail, refer to the evaluation checklist (teaching) at the end of this unit.

## Topics

| | |
|---|---|
| **THE WATER CYCLE** | |
| **HOMES** | Animal homes<br>The seaside |
| **ISLANDS / MOUNTAINS** | How they are formed |
| **THE PLANET EARTH** | Mining and quarrying |

## Cross-curricular links

| | |
|---|---|
| **ART** | Simulating a mountain or an island by adding material to a suitable rock<br>Pebble pictures; finding pictures in the quartz veins running through rocks |
| **GEOGRAPHY** | The formation of rocks and the time-scales involved<br>Water availability and use<br>Weathering and erosion<br>Extracting materials from the environment |
| **HISTORY** | Minerals which used to provide essentials such as tools, fuel and shelter; some gave their name to an age, such as the Iron Age |

## Classroom materials

The following *Nelson Science* materials support this unit:

**Picture Resource Book 1**

- cover – lightning damage
- p.4 – sandy soil stabilised by plant roots (Arizona)
- p.5 – granite shattered by frost (Swiss Alps)
- p.21 – sand dunes showing a wind-formed landscape

**Picture Resource Book 3**

- cover – Stonehenge deteriorating over the centuries
- p.4 – compare the structure of the soil with Book 1, pages 4, 5 and 21
- p.5, 6, 19 – the location of different minerals
- p.7 — the erosion of chalk cliffs; note the wave-cut pattern at the base, and the stack and arch on the headland
- p.8 – the erosion of sedimentary rocks, showing the layering (stratification), and how massive pressure has caused folding (Utah, USA)
- p.9 – the erosion of a cliff face
- p.14 – the effects of weathering (air pollution) on houses

**Science Explorers**

- **Carrying Out Surveys 1, 2 and 3**
- **Experimenting 1, 2 and 3**
- **Problem Solving 1, 2 and 3**

## Related units

### Units in the Teacher's Classroom Manual (Key Stage 2)

- The local environment and beyond - Unit 4
- Measuring the weather - Unit 9

### Units in the Teacher's Classroom Manual (Key Stage 1)

- Natural materials found in the locality: stones, rocks, soil - Unit 18

## Resources and equipment

- magnifying glasses
- a variety of rocks, collected from the area near the school and further afield
- tools to aid collection, for example, a trowel
- an auger (or a tin can with the edges taped) to collect soil samples without compressing them
- a large waterproofed tray and a watering can
- weighing machines
- a set of identical tall transparent containers
- at least one garden sieve, ideally a set of graded soil sieves
- a disposable glass container with a tightly fitting lid
- coloured tissue paper
- goggles

### Safety

Ensure that the children:

- take care when breaking rock; if this is necessary, place samples in a strong sealed bag such as an old handbag before hammering
- wear goggles if there is any danger of rock fragments flying off
- take care when opening containers where freezing has caused fractures

## Starting points

### The school environment

- a rock collection, including sedimentary, igneous and metamorphic rocks
- the effects of weathering on the school buildings
- 'sun bleaching' when old displays are taken down from the wall
- the power of plant roots to break up tarmac and walls in or around the playground

### The social environment

- holiday photographs showing differently coloured soils, sand, hills, mountains, flatlands and other geological features
- glass souvenirs filled with coloured sand from, for example, Alum Bay (Isle of Wight)
- jewellery
- old buildings or statues which show the effects of weathering
- the use of minerals in the home; for example, borax is used in soaps, detergents and weedkiller

### Further afield

- a visit to a mining museum, a quarry, a church (especially one with gravestones), or the prehistoric ('dinosaur') section of a museum
- a visit to the seashore to observe strata, reflecting that some beaches are sandy, some are pebbly or with rocky shelves, and some are backed by dunes or cliffs

Also see 'Making connections'.

## Asking questions

### I wonder whether ...

- **all rocks were formed in the same way?**
- **all walls can support plant life?**
- **all minerals are extracted from the Earth in the same way?**
- **we can date fossils?**
- **we can sort soils into types?**
- **the weather affects materials?**

## Gathering information

### Carrying out surveys

**Children:**

- **find out about the different ways in which rocks are formed (sedimentary, igneous and metamorphic)**
- **find out what walls are made of; are the materials natural or manufactured, and how does this affect plant life?**
- **find out about the main methods of extracting minerals:**
  - **floating minerals out (panning)**
  - **digging, underground or from the surface**
  - **evaporating**
  - **forcing out after melting in hot steam**
- **find out about fossils: what they are, and how and when they were formed**
- **compare soils from different locations; collect as many as possible, and devise 'fair tests' to show how they differ**
- **consider the effects of weathering**

## Asking questions

### What happens if ...

- rain falls on rocks instead of soil?
- vinegar is dropped on to stones?
- solutions of minerals are evaporated very slowly?

### Can I find a way to ...

- make an identification key to sort our rock collection?
- show how freezing and warming break up stones?
- demonstrate erosion by water?

## Gathering information

### Experimenting

**Children:**

- observe the ways in which different natural materials absorb water
- test for 'fizzing' which will show that the stone is a carbonate, and record their results
- make saturated solutions of appropriate minerals (salt and sugar, for example) and then leave the crystals to 'grow'

### Solving practical problems

**Children:**

- collect rocks and stones locally, stipulating a size rule, for example, 'smaller than a 10p' coin; they then think about 'fair tests' which they could use to classify the stones, such as tests for hardness, lustre, colour and weight
- fill an appropriate container to the brim with water, replacing the tight lid or stopper; then wrap the container and place it in the freezer
- make a 'mountain' of soil or sand; using a sprinkler or a watering can, they simulate rain and observe the rivulets

Examples of ways in which these ideas have been developed in the classroom are provided on pages 167–171.

## Handling information

- Encourage systematic listing and recording of data:
  - frequency tables
  - bar charts
- Encourage searching for patterns in data.
- Encourage written and/or oral reporting skills as appropriate.

- Encourage the use of a limited technical vocabulary in communicating findings and ideas.

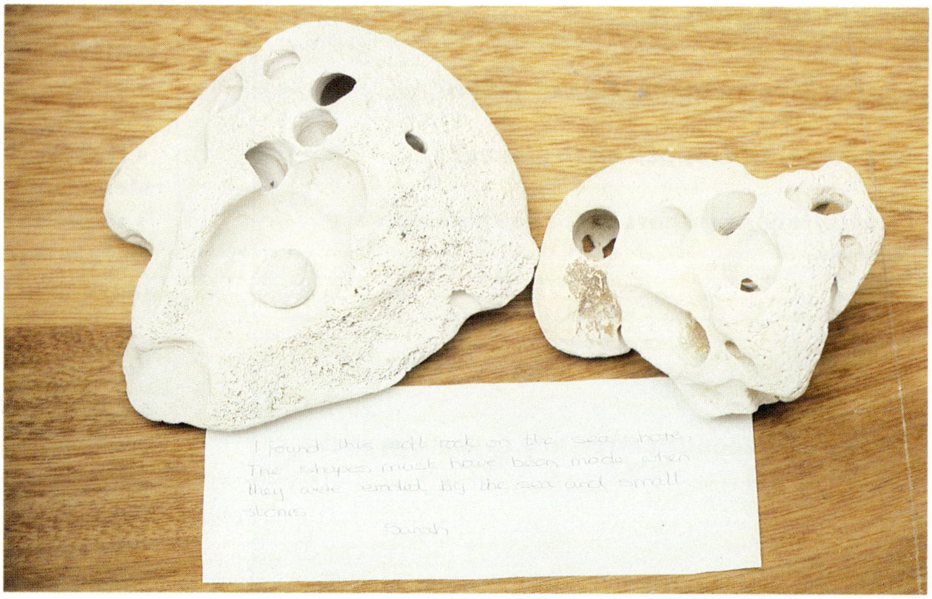


- Encourage the interpretation of data, and evaluation against the demands of the problem.

## Review points

The following are useful talking points:

### Our investigations

- new vocabulary we learned; for example: *volume, weight, lustre, transparent, translucent, opaque, erosion, weathering, expansion, contraction, crystal, impervious, permeable, igneous, metamorphic, sedimentary*; can we add to our definitions?
- the questions we raised that we answered, and those we must leave unanswered
- the variables we controlled, and those we should have or would like to have controlled
- the new equipment we used, or skills we learned; were we successful? do we need more practice?
- any patterns we noticed in the data or tentative hypotheses we made

### Making connections

- variations in the Earth's surface – for example, deserts, deep valleys, tall mountains, large caves – and what they might indicate about the nature of the rocks
- the Moh scale, named after a German mineralogist who ranked common rocks according to their hardness
- burst water pipes in winter and the need for lagging
- water mains buried underground to prevent frost damage
- dredging machines; where does the sediment come from?
- DIY shops selling different kinds of paint for protecting buildings from severe weather
- sand blasting as a method of cleaning buildings
- coal as a fossil fuel

## Investigations

### I wonder whether ...

- **all rocks were formed in the same way?**

Children observe igneous rocks such as granite, formed when molten rock cooled thousands of millions of years ago, and metamorphic rocks, such as marble, formed when these rocks were subjected to great heat and pressure. Sedimentary rocks such as sandstone were formed from fragments of both kinds; others, such as limestone, were composed of sea creatures.

Children can reflect on the differences between the rocks, and the different ways in which they are used.

Find out about volcanoes and earthquakes, and how these have affected the landscape.

- **all walls can support plant life?**

By investigating the porosity, hardness, texture and composition of the material, children can increase their understanding of the conditions necessary for plants to grow.

- **all minerals are extracted from the Earth in the same way?**

Children could try 'panning' as a method of extraction; it is advisable to use a hosepipe outside, rather than risk clogging the sink! Attractive pebbles can be 'extracted' from a flower bed in this way. Children may reflect that it is unlikely that anyone has admired their 'find' in thousands of millions of years. (Unusual larger rocks could form the centrepiece of a moss garden; see Unit 7.)

Coal and rock salt are dug from underground mines.

Ores, or rocks containing particular minerals, may simply be removed from deposits near the surface, as in opencast mining.

Sulphur is mined by sinking shafts into deposits, and then melting the sulphur with hot steam and forcing it to the surface with compressed air.

Minerals such as salt, borax and magnesium are extracted from sea water by evaporation. Children could set up their own 'extraction plant' using salt, and find the most effective conditions for rapid extraction.

- **we can date fossils?**

Plaster of Paris applied in layers coloured with food dye can give some idea of how fossil impressions are made, but not of the forces and time scales involved. See Unit 7.

- **we can sort soils into types?**

Collect soil samples, using an auger to avoid compressing them.

To compare the sizes of the particles, the samples can either be rubbed through graded sieves or shaken in tall transparent containers and left to stand for several days. The thickness of the different layers of particles can then be measured.

Organic matter tends to float on the top in this experiment, giving a rough guide to humus levels.

To compare moisture content, spread soil samples of equal weight to the same thickness on identical trays. Leave them in the same place to dry. When all the samples are dry to the touch (days later), weigh them again to compare the amounts of weight lost.

To find the volume of air in a sample, take a known volume of soil (50 $cm^3$) and add a known volume of water to it (50 $cm^3$). Shake well. The difference between the anticipated total volume (100 $cm^3$) and the actual volume gives a measure of the quantity of air in the sample.

- **the weather affects materials?**

Children may have observed the fading of coloured paper used for mounting their work on the classroom walls. They could devise an experiment based on the fading of coloured tissue paper over time to compare the amounts of sunlight falling on different parts of their classroom.

Collect evidence of deterioration due to weather effects in paintwork, some plastics and stonework, and send for relevant information from the building industry.

## What happens if ...

- **rain falls on rocks instead of soil?**

Children devise a fair test, using water with a touch of colouring in it and a dropper, to find out which surfaces allow water to soak in and which do not.

Some (impervious) rocks do not allow water to soak in; how does this help to explain the appearance of springs, or the existence of wells?

- **vinegar is dropped on to stones?**

This is a way of determining the origins of the rocks. If they are calcareous (derived from shells), they will fizz in acid.

- **solutions of minerals are evaporated very slowly?**

Patience is needed to dissolve as much of the substance, for example, sugar or salt, as the water will take. Don't therefore be tempted to use too much water. Children will discover that the slower the evaporation, the larger the crystals. They could find out about more elaborate techniques if the appropriate chemicals – alum, copper sulphate – are available.

This work could lead to (first-hand or secondary source) investigations into the formation of other mineral crystals, for example, amethyst, ruby and diamond.

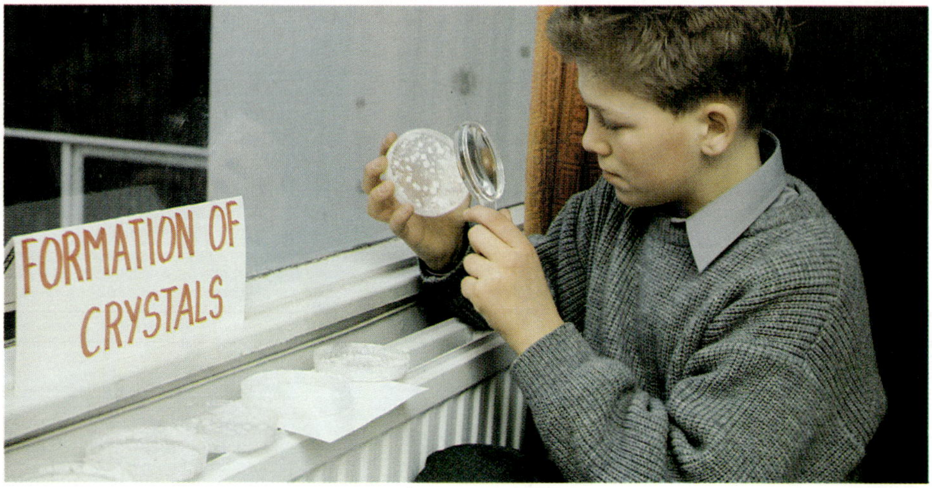

## Can I find a way to ...

**• make an identification key to sort our rock collection?**

Children could construct their own scale of:

– colour; does the pebble leave a coloured streak on a white tile?

– hardness; which scratches easily with a fingernail, coin or file?

– shininess (lustre, or the ability to reflect light)

– transparency/translucency/opacity; can you see through the pebble?

– weight

– warmth; rocks which feel warm are good insulators as they do not take the heat away from your finger

– porosity; drop a single drop of water on the pebble and observe

**• show how freezing and warming break up stones?**

Children may doubt that weathering could break up granite blocks.

This can be demonstrated convincingly by filling a glass bottle with water, wrapping it (for safety) and freezing it. Observe the pieces after freezing!

**• demonstrate erosion by water?**

Use waterproofed trays in the classroom, or extend the work to see whether plant cover or the steepness of a slope affect soil erosion or deposition.

From secondary sources or visits, find out about the problems posed by deposition in river mouths, harbours and canals.

**Unit .......................** **Date .......................**

# Teaching

**Have the children been provided with opportunities to:**

- work on questions or problems which they have accepted as their own? ☐
- develop their skills of exploration and investigation? ☐

See AT 1 evaluation checklist (page 11).

**Has the work pupils were engaged in allowed them to:**

PS 9
- investigate natural materials such as:
  - rocks? ☐
  - minerals? ☐
  - soils? ☐
- sort them according to simple criteria? ☐
- relate them to their uses and origins using books and other sources? ☐
- become aware of the local distribution of:
  - sands? ☐
  - soils? ☐
  - rocks? ☐
- observe, through urban or rural fieldwork, how weather affects natural materials, including plants, in their surroundings, and how soil develops? ☐
- consider the major geological events which change the surface of the Earth? ☐

PS 6
- work with a number of different everyday materials, grouping them according to their characteristics, similarities and differences? ☐

PS 2
- explore the range of extinct life forms preserved as fossils, using:
  - secondary sources? ☐
  - specimens (if possible)? ☐

**Unit** ........................ **Date** ........................

## Learning

**Using investigations based on this unit, have the children demonstrated that they:**

**Level 2**

AT 6 • (can) recognise important similarities and differences, including hardness, flexibility and transparency, in the characteristics of materials? ☐

AT 9 • (can) sort natural materials into broad groups according to observable features? ☐

**Level 3**

AT 9 • (can) describe from their own observations some of the effects of weathering on buildings and on the landscape? ☐

• know that air is all around us? ☐

• understand how weathering of rocks leads to the formation of different types of soil? ☐

• (can) give an account of an investigation of some natural material (rock or soil)? ☐

AT 4 • know that some life forms became extinct a long time ago and others more recently? ☐

AT 6 • know that some materials occur naturally while many are made from raw materials? ☐

• (can) list the similarities and differences in a variety of everyday materials? ☐

**Level 4**

AT 2 • understand that plants and animals can be preserved as fossils in different ways? ☐

AT 6 • (can) make comparisons between materials on the basis of simple properties, strength, hardness, flexibility and solubility? ☐

• (can) relate knowledge of these properties to the everyday use of materials? ☐

• know that solids and liquids have 'weight' which can be measured and, also, occupy a definite volume which can be measured? ☐

**Level 5**

AT 9 • know that landscapes are formed by a number of agents including Earth movements? ☐

– weathering? ☐

– erosion? ☐

– and deposition? ☐

– and that these act over different time scales? ☐

AT 6 • (can) give an account of the various techniques for separating and purifying mixtures? ☐

See AT 1 evaluation checklist (page 11).

# UNIT 13 EVERYDAY MATERIALS

## Opportunities for learning

Working from this unit, children will be developing their investigative skills and their knowledge and understanding of:

- the properties of materials, and the way in which these determine the uses of the materials and form the basis of their classification

For greater detail, refer to the evaluation checklist (teaching) at the end of this unit.

## Topics

| | |
|---|---|
| **STRUCTURES** | Bridges, dams, building sites |
| **CELEBRATIONS** | Clothing<br>Cooking<br>Candles |
| **COLOUR** | Textiles |
| **FIRE** | Firefighters |
| **ENERGY** | Coal, gas, oil and water |

## Cross-curricular links

| | |
|---|---|
| **GEOGRAPHY** | Famous bridges, walls and dams; materials used in improving the quality of the environment |
| **HISTORY** | Fabrics through the ages, for example flax in Egypt and silk in China<br>The flying shuttle, the Spinning Jenny<br>Bridges, walls and pyramids and the needs they were fulfilling<br>The history of brick making |
| **MATHEMATICS** | Symmetry in the shapes of structures |

## Classroom materials

The following *Nelson Science* materials support this unit:

**Picture Resource Book 1**

- p.5 – granite
- p.8 – wood
- p.20 – icebergs; how much ice is below the surface?

**Picture Resource Book 2**

- p.1, 4, 5, 6 – the properties of different materials and their use in clothing, furniture, soft furnishings, utensils and jewellery
- p.6 – materials used for fillings
- p.20 – biodegradable and non-biodegradable materials

**Picture Resource Book 3**

- p.1 – materials used to create sound
- p.3, 6 – protective clothing
- p.10 – a suspension bridge (Golden Gate, California)
- p.11 – an iron bridge, an arch
- p.15 – woollen thread and a nylon stocking seen at high magnification
- p.16, 17, 18, 19 – timber, wool, cotton, iron ore
- p.22 – materials found in a kitchen, including magnets

**Science Explorers**

- **Carrying Out Surveys 1, 2 and 3**
- **Experimenting 1, 2 and 3**
- **Problem Solving 1, 2 and 3**

## Related units

### Units in the Teacher's Classroom Manual (Key Stage 2)

- Colour, mirrors, lenses and prisms – Unit 1
- Noise and music – Unit 2
- Circuits, switching and control – Unit 3
- Measuring the weather – Unit 9
- Movement, forces and energy – Unit 11

### Units in the Teacher's Classroom Manual (Key Stage 1)

- Everyday materials: sand, wood, metal, plastics, paper, clay, fabrics (including magnets) – Unit 20

## Resources and equipment

- a collection of natural and synthetic textiles
- a sand tray
- tongs
- a candle
- newspapers
- bulldog clips
- weights on a hook
- cocoa, curry, salt, pepper, flour, powdered milk
- plenty of clean containers for mixing, for example, cut-down lemonade bottles, yoghurt pots
- implements for measuring volume, for example, teaspoons
- access to a water supply
- plasticine
- small identical 'weights', for example, paperclips
- junk materials
- magnifying glasses
- ice balloons
- plaster of Paris

## Safety

Ensure that the children:
- observe hygiene considerations when food is being prepared for consumption
- know the dangers of using hot oil or bleach
- wear goggles and use appropriate tools when mixing plaster of Paris or concrete, and are aware of the possibility of allergic reactions
- take care when using solvents; some things which do not dissolve in water dissolve in other things
- are supervised when using naked flames and avoid substances known to cause noxious fumes, such as most plastics

## Starting points

### The school environment

- cooking (this could be subsidised by running a one-day class café)
- local newspaper articles about, for example, chip pan fires
- labels in clothes showing washing instructions
- classroom fire precautions such as a fire extinguisher or blanket

### The social environment

- cooking at home; observing changes in foods, for example melting and solidifying
- helping with DIY projects, especially where concrete, plaster, wood fillings, solder or adhesives are involved
- sorting laundry for washing and dry cleaning
- television advertisements; design fair tests to see whether their claims are true
- watching someone welding, for example, in a garage

### Further afield

- a visit to a chocolate factory, a bakery, a clothing factory (spinning, weaving) or a glass factory
- a visit to a fire station, inspecting protective clothing if possible
- a visit to a harbour; look at the plimsoll line on ships and the pulley systems on cranes
- a visit to a building site; observe the difference between load-bearing walls and partition walls
- buildings with buttresses, domes or spires; how are they built to stand up against gravity?

Also see 'Making connections'.

## Asking questions

### I wonder whether ...

- the fibres in certain textiles are natural or synthetic?
- all bridges are constructed on the same principles?
- powdered mashed potato is better value than fresh potato?

### What happens if ...

- I burn pieces of fabric?
- Water is added to plaster of Paris?
- I place my ice balloon in water?

### Can I find a way to ...

- show that air is a 'real' thing?
- find the strongest kind of paper?
- make a bridge to span a one-metre gap?
- construct a scale of solubility for kitchen powders?
- find out which ball is the best bouncer?
- change water from a solid into a liquid, and then into a gas?

## Gathering information

### Carrying out surveys

**Children:**

- find out about fibres and establish by observation with a magnifying glass that textiles are made up of fibres
- investigate bridges, locally or further afield; find out what loads they carry, and what materials are used in their construction
- survey the many different forms in which potatoes are sold; construct a fair test to determine value for money, remembering seasonal variations in the price of fresh potatoes

### Experimenting

**Children:**

- make predictions and then burn small strips of fabric of identical size, using tongs and a candle set in a sand tray
- consult the instructions on the packet for the ratio of powder to liquid
- observe, record and make predictions about the ice

### Solving practical problems

**Children:**

- consider a collection of clean containers, reflecting that we would refer to them as 'empty', or as having `nothing' in them; devise some simple ways of showing that 'something' must be in them
- construct apparatus to test paper strips of the same size, using increasing weights
- build bridges based on their experience of bridge construction and testing for the strongest paper; they should limit the variables, and then test the bridges
- predict whether the various powders will dissolve in cold water (extend to hot if appropriate), and then design a fair test
- design a fair test, considering the way the balls will be dropped and the surface on to which they are dropped
- consider whether the changes are permanent

Examples of ways in which these ideas have been developed in the classroom are provided on pages 179–183.

## Handling information

- Encourage systematic listing and recording of data:
  - frequency tables

- Encourage written and/or oral reporting skills as appropriate.

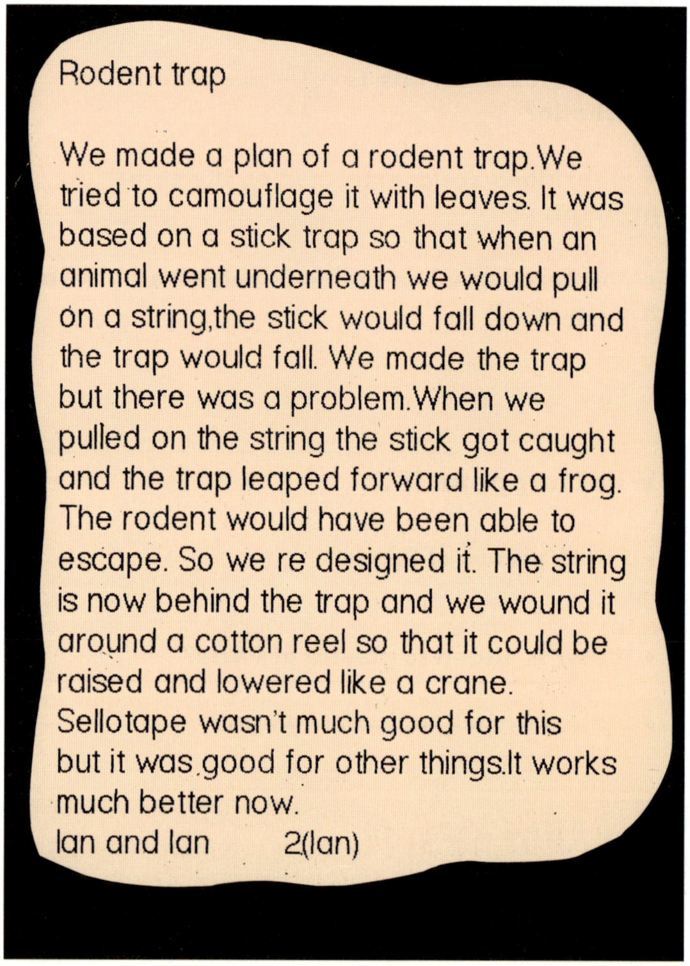

Rodent trap

We made a plan of a rodent trap.We tried to camouflage it with leaves. It was based on a stick trap so that when an animal went underneath we would pull on a string,the stick would fall down and the trap would fall. We made the trap but there was a problem.When we pulled on the string the stick got caught and the trap leaped forward like a frog. The rodent would have been able to escape. So we re designed it. The string is now behind the trap and we wound it around a cotton reel so that it could be raised and lowered like a crane. Sellotape wasn't much good for this but it was good for other things.It works much better now.

Ian and Ian 2(Ian)

  - bar charts
- Encourage searching for patterns in data.

- Encourage the use of a limited technical vocabulary in communicating findings and ideas.
- Encourage the interpretation of data, and evaluation against the demands of the problem.

## Review points

The following are useful talking points:

### Our investigations

- new vocabulary we learned; for example: *volume, weight, strength, hardness, flexibility, compressibility, solubility, solvent, freezing, boiling, water vapour, evaporation, condensation, dissolve, soluble, solid, liquid, gas, force, buoyancy, upthrust, displacement;* can we add to our definitions?
- the questions we raised that we answered, and those we must leave unanswered
- the variables we controlled, and those we should have or would like to have controlled
- the new equipment we used, or skills we learned; were we successful? do we need more practice?
- any patterns we noticed in the data or tentative hypotheses we made

### Making connections

- the use in hospitals of plaster, a material which hardens quickly through chemical change
- making clay pots; strong heat (in a kiln) is needed to change clay chemically and make it permanently hard
- concrete; the right mix is required to effect a chemical change as it sets
- the international labelling codes for textiles
- the international hazard warning symbol
- stain removal and the use of solvents
- fabric testing and standards in industry; some tests are based on the number of 'rubs' before the cloth shows signs of wear
- the 'puddling' of canals because clay is impervious
- white carbonate 'fur' inside kettles in hard water areas
- the commercial extraction of salt from the sea through evaporation (see Unit 12)
- the importance of salt to body chemistry and as a food preservative
- icebergs as a danger to shipping
- buoyancy tanks in sailing boats and submarines

## Investigations

### I wonder whether ...

- **the fibres in certain textiles are natural or synthetic?**

Children find out about:

– natural fibres such as cotton, flax, wool, silk, coconut and asbestos

– synthetic fibres invented by chemical engineers, including nylon and acrylic

Try to find actual examples of each textile, relating them to properties such as warmth, waterproofing and strength.

- **all bridges are constructed on the same principles?**

Children could consider suspension bridges, box girders and simple arches. What holds each one up; which has the strongest construction; where are the weakest points? Children could invent or copy a design, concentrating on constructing models which work.

- **powdered mashed potato is better value than fresh potato?**

Children cost and weigh crisps, fresh potato, dried and rehydrated mash and frozen oven-ready chips. Are taste, smell and appearance important? What are the criteria for value?

## What happens if …

- **I burn small pieces of fabric?**

Children time how long the samples take to burn using a stop-clock. Observe and record the colour and nature of the flame, the smoke and the ash. Which material is the most flammable? Which materials do firefighters use?

- **water is added to plaster of Paris?**

Feel the heat of the chemical reaction, and time how long it takes to set hard. Can it be changed back? What happens if different amounts of water are used?

(Link this to work on bark prints, fossils or animal tracks where plaster of Paris is needed.)

- **I place my ice balloon in water?**

Make an ice balloon by filling a balloon with water, freezing it until solid and then removing the balloon.

Children will raise so many questions that they may need a second session to consider floating and sinking.

## Can I find a way to ...

- **show that air is a 'real' thing?**

Push a dry cotton wool pad or tissues into the base of a transparent beaker. Children hold it upside down, and then press it vertically into a bowl of water. Predict whether the material will be wet when the beaker is lifted vertically out again. Why isn't it wet?

Make a 'watering can' using a plastic container with a lid. Make a small hole in the base and multiple holes in the lid, fill it with water and invert it over a bowl. A finger blocking the hole will stop the sprinkle.

Using an ear dropper and a two-litre plastic lemonade bottle, (or a manufactured 'cartesian diver' in a corked bottle), show that air can be squeezed.

- **find the strongest kind of paper?**

Decide whether to tear the strips vertically or horizontally. (A magnifying glass can be used to decide why this is important.)

Fix a bulldog clip on one end of each strip, hook it to a stand, and add weights to the strip.

What happens if you run a wet finger across the newspaper strip under tension?

- **make a bridge to span a one-metre gap?**

Rules can be made, for example: use a maximum of two newspapers and sellotape only; the bridge must allow a given dumper truck to be pulled across.

**• construct a scale of solubility for kitchen powders?**

A fair test will involve controlling variables such as the amount of the substance used, the number of stirs and the temperature of the water. Will some substances dissolve better in hot water? Make observations as to whether the substance floats or sinks, is crystalline, or smells.

Try using other solvents but remember that some dangerous powders can be deceptive in appearance.

**• find out which ball is the best bouncer?**

Discuss what is meant by 'best'. Does the size of the ball make any difference? Predict the results. Can the results be used to recommend which balls can and cannot be used near windows?

Consider bouncing the same ball on different surfaces and predicting how and at what angle it will bounce.

**• change water from a solid into a liquid, and then into a gas?**

Children could discover the melting point of water, but boiling water is not recommended in the classroom.

Notice how ice floats on water, and consider why this is a danger to shipping.

**Unit ........................** **Date ........................**

## Teaching

**Have the children been provided with opportunities to:**

- work on questions or problems which they have accepted as their own? ☐
- develop their skills of exploration and investigation? ☐

See AT 1 evaluation checklist (page 11).

**Has the work the pupils were engaged in allowed them to:**

PS 6
- work with a number of different everyday materials, grouping them according to their characteristics, similarities and differences? ☐
- explore the origins of different materials through secondary sources and see how they are used? ☐
- investigate and measure:
  - – mass (weight)? ☐
  - – volume? ☐
  - – strength? ☐
  - – hardness? ☐
  - – flexibility? ☐
  - – compressibility? ☐
  - – solubility? ☐
  - – the changes brought about by heating and cooling? ☐
- explore chemical changes in a number of everyday materials, for example:
  - – mix plaster of Paris? ☐
  - – make concrete? ☐
  - – fire clay? ☐
- relate the ways in which materials are used to the properties they have investigated? ☐
- learn about the dangers associated with the use of everyday materials such as bleach and hot oil? ☐

PS 13
- investigate the changes which occur when familiar substances are heated and cooled? ☐

**Unit** ........................ **Date** ........................

# Learning

**Using investigations based on this unit, have the children demonstrated that they:**

**Level 1**

AT 6 • (can) describe familiar and unfamiliar objects in terms of simple properties, for example, shape, colour, texture, and describe how they behave when they are, for example, squashed and stretched? ☐

**Level 2**

AT 6 • (can) recognise important similarities and differences, including hardness, flexibility and transparency, in the characteristics of materials? ☐

• (can) group materials according to their characteristics? ☐

• know that heating or cooling materials can cause them to melt or solidify or change permanently? ☐

AT 9 • (can) sort natural materials into broad groups according to observable features? ☐

**Level 3**

AT 6 • know that some materials occur naturally while many are made from raw materials? ☐

• (can) list the similarities and differences in a variety of everyday materials? ☐

AT 9 • know that air is all around us? ☐

At 13 • know that the temperature is a measure of how hot (or cold) things are? ☐

**Level 4**

AT 6 • (can) make comparisons between materials on the basis of simple properties, strength, hardness, flexibility and solubility? ☐

• (can) relate knowledge of these properties to the everyday use of materials? ☐

• know that solids and liquids have 'weight' which can be measured? ☐

– and, also, occupy a definite volume which can be measured? ☐

• understand the sequence of changes of state that results from heating or cooling? ☐

• (can) classify materials into solids, liquids and gases on the basis of their properties? ☐

AT 13 • (can) measure temperature using a thermometer? ☐

• (can) give an account of changes that occur when familiar substances are heated and cooled? ☐

See AT 1 evaluation checklist (page 11).

# Section 3
# Planning Science

## Approach A

This approach to planning allows the teacher to exploit the potential of a cross-curricular or thematic approach. The teacher can see the units in the context of the whole curriculum and choose activities within the units which will support learning in a given topic.

## Approach B

By using the themes and units as a planning framework, the teacher is released from the task of continually cross-checking coverage of the **Programme of Study**. If all the units are covered during **Key Stage 2** the requirements of the **National Curriculum** will be met. The record sheets on pages 190 and 191 provide help with record keeping.

## Following Approach A

This section provides a strategy for identifying learning outcomes and choosing topics to support them. By following this strategy teachers will be able to ensure that during **Key Stage 2** children are provided with a balanced set of science experiences which cover the full range of the **National Curriculum Programmes of Study** and **Attainment Targets**.

### Overview of the approach

**Step 1**

- Select topics

All the teachers in a school should collaborate to identify areas of study to use as vehicles for children's learning across the curriculum. These areas of study might be topics, themes or projects, such as 'Clothes', or units of work based on a resource, such as 'The school pond'. For the sake of simplicity, the term 'topic' is used throughout this section.

Points to consider when choosing topics:

- the children's needs and interests, and the appropriateness of the topic to their experience and stage of development. In particular, consider the opportunities the topic could provide for expanding children's awareness of cultural and ethnic diversity and equal opportunities.
- the children's previous curriculum experience. Consider the sections of the **Programmes of Study** covered by previous topics.
- the available resources. Consider the range and quality of appropriate objects and materials which can be made available for children to handle and work with. In particular, consider the season, the visits which can be arranged, the stories and poems which can be provided, and the potential for the use of information technology.
- cross-curricular links. Consider the scope which the topic provides for a wide-ranging selection of activities embracing aspects of the other foundation subjects and the broader school curriculum.

**Step 2**

- **Identify the potential for science experiences**
- **Record this potential**

Having selected your topics, use the flow diagram (pages 188-189) to identify which themes and units might be covered by your chosen topics. Record this potential on the class record sheet (page 190). Tick in pencil the units which appear to contain appropriate investigations.

**Step 3**

- **Follow up the potential by:**
  - **using the summary record of children's previous science experience (see page 191)**
  - **reading the 'starting points' in each identified unit**
- **Record any units as 'definites' in ink on the class record sheet (see page 190)**

Read the questions in the selected units to choose which investigations you might use to provide children with experiences within your chosen topic.

Points to consider include:

- whether this topic gives the best context for the units you have identified
- whether this is the best stage at which to present the ideas covered by the unit. For example, attempting investigations in Unit 10 before Unit 1 has been covered may be a futile exercise.
- how your topic will extend the children's experience if it covers units they have visited before

**Step 4**

- **Do the planned work in the classroom**

**Step 5**

- **Record the details of experiences as they are provided**

During the classroom work, record the **Statements of Attainment** and the aspects of the **Programme of Study** covered by the unit on the evaluation checklists at the end of each unit. You may find it valuable to record the actual investigations which the children have worked on within each unit.

This detailed record will be a valuable resource for other teachers, who will duly be able to take account of the work you have done with the children in their planning.

**Step 6**

- **Record a summary of these experiences on the school record sheet (page 191) at agreed times through the year**

If this approach is adopted by the whole school it will be possible to build up a summative record relating to a particular year group of pupils with information to ensure a balanced coverage of the science curriculum.

## Identifying opportunities

Does your topic provide the children with opportunities to find out about:

| Themes | | Units and possible areas of work |
|---|---|---|
| Light (pp 14–27) | ☐ Yes → | Colour, mirrors, lenses and prisms<br>– reflections<br>– shadows<br>– magnifying<br>– coloured light<br>– light and materials |
| No ↓ | | |
| Sound (pp 28–43) | ☐ Yes → | Noise and music<br>– making musical instruments<br>– vibrations<br>– how sound travels<br>– noise pollution<br>– sound insulation<br>– the storage, retrieval and transmission of sound |
| No ↓ | | |
| Batteries, buzzers and bulbs (pp 44–57) | ☐ Yes → | Circuits, switching and control<br>– powered models<br>– energy transfer<br>– logic gates<br>– magnetism and magnetic effects<br>– switches for a variety of uses |
| No ↓ | | |
| How people change the environment (pp 58–69) | ☐ Yes → | The local environment and beyond<br>– pollution<br>– recycling<br>– waste disposal<br>– energy resources<br>– water purification |
| No ↓ | | |
| Themselves and others and how to keep healthy (pp 70–83) | ☐ Yes → | Our bodies<br>– healthy living<br>– individual differences<br>– the senses<br>– growth<br>– circulation<br>– reproduction<br>– movement |

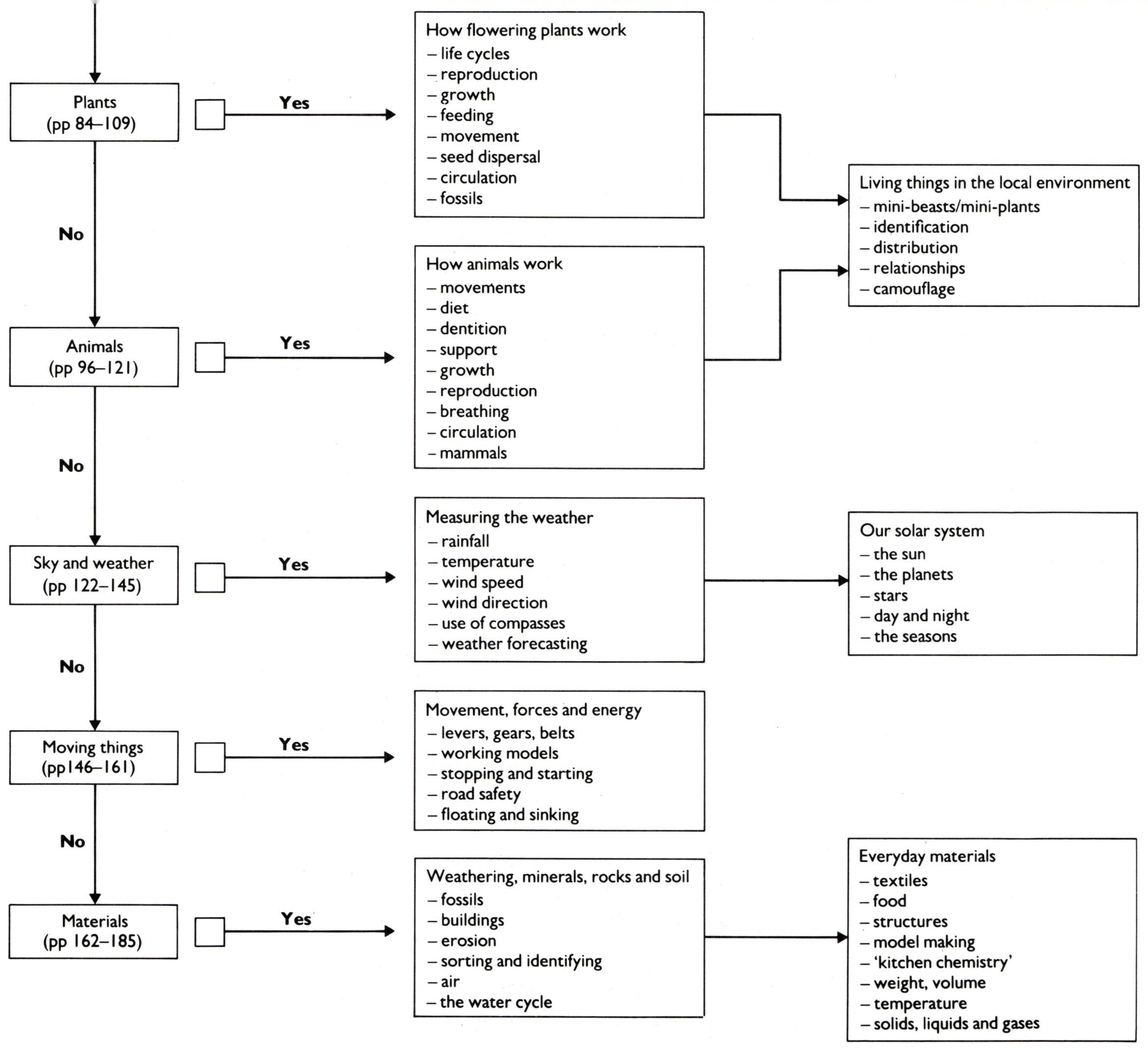
Plants
(pp 84–109)
Yes
How flowering plants work
– life cycles
– reproduction
– growth
– feeding
– movement
– seed dispersal
– circulation
– fossils
No
Animals
(pp 96–121)
Yes
How animals work
– movements
– diet
– dentition
– support
– growth
– reproduction
– breathing
– circulation
– mammals
Living things in the local environment
– mini-beasts/mini-plants
– identification
– distribution
– relationships
– camouflage
No
Sky and weather
(pp 122–145)
Yes
Measuring the weather
– rainfall
– temperature
– wind speed
– wind direction
– use of compasses
– weather forecasting
Our solar system
– the sun
– the planets
– stars
– day and night
– the seasons
No
Moving things
(pp146–161)
Yes
Movement, forces and energy
– levers, gears, belts
– working models
– stopping and starting
– road safety
– floating and sinking
No
Materials
(pp 162–185)
Yes
Weathering, minerals, rocks and soil
– fossils
– buildings
– erosion
– sorting and identifying
– air
– the water cycle
Everyday materials
– textiles
– food
– structures
– model making
– 'kitchen chemistry'
– weight, volume
– temperature
– solids, liquids and gases

## Class record sheet

**Class** ____________ **Year** ________

| **Finding out about ...** | | **Autumn term** | | **Spring term** | | **Summer term** | |
|---|---|---|---|---|---|---|---|
| | | **Topics** | | **Topics** | | **Topics** | |
| Light | Colour, mirrors, lenses and prisms | | | | | | |
| Sound | Noise and music | | | | | | |
| Batteries, buzzers and bulbs | Circuits, switching and control | | | | | | |
| How people change the environment | The local enviroment and beyond | | | | | | |
| Themselves and others and how to keep healthy | Our bodies | | | | | | |
| Plants | How flowering plants work | | | | | | |
| | Living things in the local environment | | | | | | |
| Animals | How animals work | | | | | | |
| Sky and weather | Measuring the weather | | | | | | |
| | Our solar system | | | | | | |
| Moving things | Movement, forces and energy | | | | | | |
| Materials | Weathering, minerals, rocks and soil | | | | | | |
| | Everyday materials | | | | | | |

# School record sheet

| Finding out about ... | | Key Stage 2 | | | | | | | | | | | |
|---|---|---|---|---|---|---|---|---|---|---|---|---|---|
| | | Year 3 | | | Year 4 | | | Year 5 | | | Year 6 | | |
| | | Autumn | Spring | Summer | Autumn | Spring | Summer | Autumn | Spring | Summer | Autumn | Spring | Summer |
| Light | Colour, mirrors, lenses and prisms | | | | | | | | | | | | |
| Sound | Noise and music | | | | | | | | | | | | |
| Batteries, buzzers and bulbs | Circuits, switching and control | | | | | | | | | | | | |
| How people change the environment | The local environment and beyond | | | | | | | | | | | | |
| Themselves and others and how to keep healthy | Our bodies | | | | | | | | | | | | |
| Plants | How flowering plants work | | | | | | | | | | | | |
| | Living things in the local environment | | | | | | | | | | | | |
| Animals | How animals work | | | | | | | | | | | | |
| Sky and weather | Measuring the weather | | | | | | | | | | | | |
| | Our solar system | | | | | | | | | | | | |
| Moving things | Movement, forces and energy | | | | | | | | | | | | |
| Materials | Weathering, minerals, rocks and soil | | | | | | | | | | | | |
| | Everyday materials | | | | | | | | | | | | |

# Appendix A

Examples of data handling programs

| Program | Details | Supplier |
|---|---|---|
| *Branch* | A binary tree database which helps children to see similarities between groups of objects | MESU<br>Unit 6<br>Sir William Lyons Road<br>Science Park<br>University of Warwick<br>Coventry<br>CV4 7EZ |
| *Datashow* | A simple graphing program which children can use to enter and sort data and see it displayed as a table, bar chart or pie chart | Hoddle, Doyle and Meadow Ltd<br>Old Head Road<br>Elseham<br>Bishop's Stortford<br>Hertfordshire<br>CS22 6JN |
| *Our Facts* | A straightforward database which allows creation and interrogation of files on any topic | |
| *First Facts* | An easy-to-use database requiring a minimum of keystrokes to enter and review data | Resource<br>Exeter Road<br>Off Coventry Road<br>Doncaster<br>South Yorkshire<br>DN2 4PY |
| *Junior Find* | A simplified version of *Find* which is an introduction to the topic of information handling | |
| *Grass* | A simple integrated retrieval and graphing program | Newman Software<br>Newman College<br>Genners Lane<br>Burtley Green<br>Birmingham<br>B32 3NT |

# Appendix B

Technical vocabulary
(numbers refer to the units in which the words occur)

# Index of topics

(numbers refer to the units where topic links are possible)